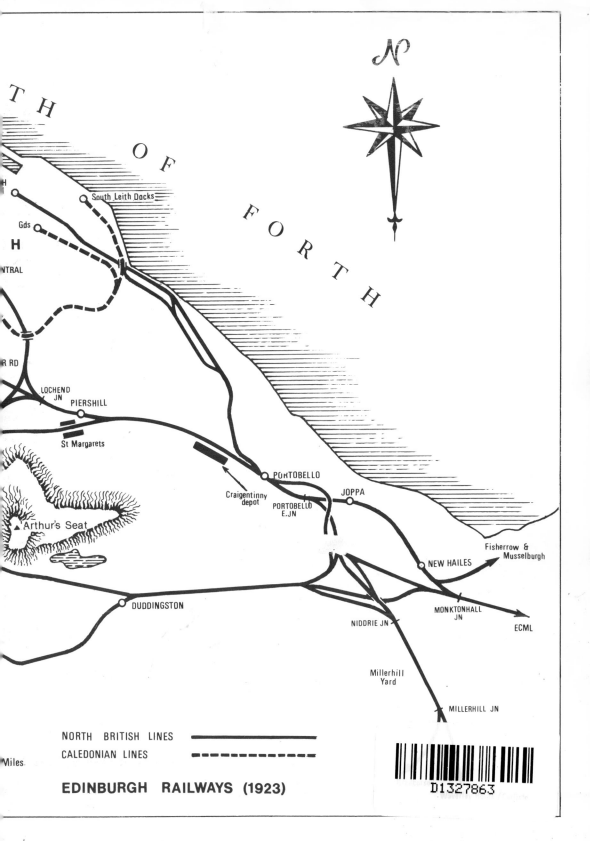

EDINBURGH RAILWAYS (1923)

NORTH BRITISH LINES ——————
CALEDONIAN LINES --------------

Miles.

South Leith Docks
Gds
NTRAL
H
R RD
LOCHEND JN
PIERSHILL
St Margarets
Craigentinny depot
▲ Arthur's Seat
PORTOBELLO
PORTOBELLO E.JN
JOPPA
Fisherrow & Musselburgh
NEW HAILES
DUDDINGSTON
NIDDRIE JN
MONKTONHALL JN
ECML
Millerhill Yard
MILLERHILL JN

RAIL CENTRES:
EDINBURGH

RAIL CENTRES:
EDINBURGH

A.J. MULLAY

LONDON
IAN ALLAN LTD

First published 1991

ISBN 0 7110 1983 5

© Ian Allan Ltd 1991

Published by Ian Allan Ltd, Shepperton, Surrey; and printed by Ian Allan Printing Ltd at their works at Coombelands in Runnymede, England

Endpapers:
Edinburgh's railways at Grouping, 1923.

Below:
As part of the Forth Bridge centenary celebrations on 4 March 1990, photographers and the media were taken on to the bridge behind Class 47/4 No 47835 *Windsor Castle* to witness the unveiling of a new plaque by the Earl of Elgin & Kincardine and Sir Robert Reid CBE, and to see Class A4 Pacific No 60009 *Osprey* (ex *Union of South Africa*) steam across with a special train for invited guests. *Brian Morrison*

Acknowledgements
The author wishes to acknowledge his gratitude for assistance given him in the writing of this book by Douglas Park and Jimmy Allan of ScotRail, and by fellow enthusiasts Mike Macdonald, John Robertson, W. S. Sellar and Hamish Stevenson. A particular word of thanks is due to Mr W. E. Boyd for making his collection of archival photographs so freely available. The staffs of the National Library of Scotland, Edinburgh City Libraries (particularly the Edinburgh Room), and Mitchell Library Glasgow are thanked. The Scottish Record Office offered its usual, totally unique, service to this researcher. The editorial guidance of Gavin Booth is also gratefully acknowledged.

Previous page left:
In the shadow of the remaining part of the former Calton Gaol, a Metro-Cammell DMU on the 16.35 to North Berwick in June 1977. *Brian Morrison*

Previous page right:
Waverley's West End in 1930, showing both the manually-operated box and, on the right, the site of the mid-1930s electrically-operated cabin (since closed). An ominous sight on the Waverley Bridge in the middle distance are the tops of SMT motor buses which provided the railways in the Lothians with a powerful and well-organised competitor from as early as 1906 onwards. *Scottish Record Office*

Contents

Introduction

Edinburgh is a city with steel tracks at its heart. Even in such a central location as Princes Street Gardens, the rumble of a passing express reminds tourists and citizens alike that a railway runs through the centre of Scotland's capital, bisecting the Gardens and tunnelling under the art galleries on the historic Mound — and all this literally in the shadow of Europe's most famous castle.

> 'Edinburgh cannot be called a place of much trade or manufacture, being chiefly supported by persons in the law and medical professions, especially the former.'

While this view of Edinburgh, published by George Measom in 1859, is perhaps a little exaggerated in the disproportionate importance it places on the professions, nevertheless it carries some justification. The Scottish capital has never attracted the heavy industry which characterised, and to some extent disfigured, the West of Scotland, despite the reasonable propinquity of coal, iron ores, and the transport sinews to transport them in the Edinburgh area.

One hundred and twenty years after Measom, Mike Macdonald was writing in *Modern Railways*:

> 'Edinburgh is primarily a "service"/tourist centre, with more than two-thirds of its employment in administration, shopping, tourism etc, and its main rail traffic flows are not surprisingly, passenger flows.'

During the 19th century the Industrial Revolution increasingly assigned Edinburgh an administrative role, with banking and insurance rapidly gaining in importance within the city, which retained its function as the centre for the nation's institutions —

Below:
Steel tracks at the heart of a city. The railway cuts through the heart of Edinburgh in Princes Street Gardens. To the right towers Edinburgh Castle rock, to the left the Gardens and Princes Street itself. Peppercorn 'A2' Pacific No 60530 *Sayajirao* makes an impressive sight in March 1957 as it heads the 14.15 train to Aberdeen. It has just emerged from the Mound tunnel, surmounted by the National Galleries of Scotland. *G. M. Staddon/N. E. Stead collection*

law, religion, and home of one of Europe's most important scientific universities. Those industries which grew in the city included brewing, papermaking and printing, some rubber and glass-making, with shipbuilding and associated industries in the Leith area. Electronics was a recent addition to this list, while papermaking is now almost defunct, in common with so many other industries in the present recession which has so affected the nation's manufacturing base, and diminished BR's freight revenue.

Indeed, since 1979, when Macdonald made his survey of rail traffic in Edinburgh — and its hinterland of Lothian Region — for *Modern Railways*, ScotRail has lost major freight traffic revenues in Edinburgh and its environs. Leith no longer requires steel materials for shipbuilding, gas production ceased at Granton from 1987 (the rails were lifted the previous year), no automotive products are manufactured at nearby Bathgate, seasonal potato traffic has all but vanished, and the North Sea oil boom has undergone cyclical changes. Even the number of local breweries can now be counted on the fingers of one hand in this city which was once one of Europe's major centres for beer production. Not surprisingly, freight is no longer loaded on to rail at the two once-thriving Leith Walk depots, and Portobello's Freightliner depot was closed in April 1987.

The story of Edinburgh's present-day rail system is thus very much one of passenger services. Although the Scottish capital has a busy freight depot at Leith South, the city is principally a passenger-orientated rail centre — George Measom's 1859 description was perhaps not that very far of the mark in predicting today's conditions.

Gateway to Scotland

Destination for the Railway Races of 1888 and 1901, and an engine-change point in the 1895 contest to Aberdeen, Edinburgh's railway network has always been geared to Anglo-Scottish express traffic. For most of its existence, the locally-based North British Railway scheduled its major north- and west-bound passenger trains to Aberdeen, Dundee, Perth, and Glasgow, to connect with expresses arriving at Waverley station from the south in the early mornings and evenings. Any serious unpunctuality at Peterborough or Leicester guaranteed a late departure from Waverley, and resulted in delays across Scotland from Kinross Junction to Arbroath.

The Waverley — at one time Britain's biggest station — was one of England's two major gateways into Scotland, and still is, although at the time of writing many modern IC125 services work right through to Scottish destinations north and west of the Forth. This gives Edinburgh a number of bonus points over its rival city Glasgow, in BR's eyes. The latter, although bigger and more industrialised, has no through station; trains from the West Coast main line to northern Scottish destinations have to bypass Glasgow via Cumbernauld, and exchange electric for diesel power. As if to emphasise the importance of Waverley being a combined through and terminal station — a versatility which will be examined in greater detail later — Edinburgh's other major station closed unsung in 1965.

This was Princes Street, whose highly convenient ground level situation at the heart of the city's West

Above:
This 1964 view gives some idea of the size of Princes Street station as Dalry Road-based Fairburn 4MT 2-6-4T No 42273 heads west with a lunchtime local to Kingsknowe. *G. M. Staddon/N. E. Stead collection*

End could not overcome the problems posed by its rigid terminal configuration. The far-sighted Caledonian Railway recognised this problem but its proposals to eliminate it by converting Princes Street into a through station were spectacularly doomed to failure, as will be recounted later.

So it was Waverley which entered a second century of arrivals and departures of London expresses by two quite different routes, via the existing East Coast main line from King's Cross through York and Newcastle, or via the now-closed Waverley Route and the Settle-Carlisle line to St Pancras. For many years, North Eastern and North British Atlantics stood side by side at Waverley platform ends, before the magnificent Pacifics of Sir Nigel Gresley — Edinburgh-born, incidentally — took over expresses to London by both routes. Class 40 diesels and the popular 'Deltics' were next to drown out the train announcements for intending passengers, before the new generation of High Speed Trains in 1979 all but reduced Waverley to the level of just another stop between King's Cross and Aberdeen or Inverness.

An interim stopping place it may present be, but nevertheless, Waverley is booming. In 1985, with 20,000 daily users, it recorded the highest business turnover of any Scottish station (£12 million), although Glasgow's Central and Queen Street had a higher cumulative total, as one might expect. As discussed later, the station's commercial pre-eminence in the ScotRail network is the direct result of its through configuration, but this book will not examine the Waverley uncritically. In particular its failure to serve its own hinterland will be examined, and will be compared unfavourably with Glasgow Central in this respect.

The scene has changed again with the extension of electrification to Edinburgh in 1991. The main London-Edinburgh service is now worked by IC225 electric trains, with IC125s providing the through London-Edinburgh-Aberdeen service. A new development at the time was the introduction of through electric trains between London King's Cross and Glasgow Central, via Edinburgh. This replaced the IC125s that formerly ran from Glasgow Queen Street to King's Cross, and is intended to provide additional journey opportunities between Glasgow and North of England. Through Glasgow-London passengers will still be encouraged to travel by the West Coast main line.

Leith and other links

Edinburgh has always been more than just a paradise for train spotters, anxious to 'cop namers'. So intensive was coal traffic at one time in the area of the city's environs that Train Control had to be introduced from a very early period, and an entirely new network of freight routes grafted on to the existing lines between the Lothian coalfield and the busy port of Leith. Indeed, so desperate were Lothian coalmine owners for an improved rail service between local pitheads and Leith that they threatened to build their own railway if the North British did not improve theirs!

The port of Leith was independent of Edinburgh from 1833 to 1920 and was served by no fewer than four passenger termini and a myriad of freight depots and yards. The biggest of the former passenger stations — Leith Central — once held the doubtful accolade of being Britain's biggest railway ruin, and its sad story will be examined in the detail it deserves later in this book. One of Leith's freight connections still exists into the dock area, which is more than some larger British ports can claim.

Local branch lines extended to rural communities and tiny burghs within a few miles of Princes Street's two major stations — no fewer than 12 lines at one time — guaranteeing a fascinating variety of trains, large and small, in and out of the city. Unfortunately most of these are now consigned to history, although at the time of writing, services to North Berwick and Bathgate are enjoying official favour and public patronage.

But it is ironic that one of Edinburgh's main characteristics, its reputation as an intellectual centre, may have declined because of the railway. From about 1780 to 1850 the Scottish capital was in the grip of the Enlightenment, an explosion of activity in science and the arts, centred on the city's university which was unfettered by the religious restrictions then inhibiting the growth of Oxford and Cambridge.

Edinburgh became a world centre in the fields of medicine, geology, technology, and philosophical theory. Yet by 1850 the glory was gone. Is it too much of a coincidence that by this date, train travel had put the budding career scientist within a comfortable 15hr of London, with no sea voyage or overnight stay to be endured? At least, if Edinburgh's rail connections drained the city of much of its intellectual vitality, they compensated by bringing hordes of tourists, first of all to see the countryside publicised by Edinburgh's own Sir Walter Scott, and after 1947, to enjoy the International Festival.

Edinburgh's rail links with London have always been vital to its well-being. Even as late as the mid-1950s no fewer than five morning express trains left the Scottish capital for its larger English counterpart within a 25min period, utilising three different routes.

Any description of Edinburgh's railway infrastructure must include at least a passing consideration of its roads. Probably unique among European capitals in not having a single mile of urban motorway within its centre, Edinburgh is not even directly connected to the British inter-urban motorway network.

The nearest a motorway comes to the city is the Newbridge roundabout some 10 miles west of Edinburgh, a couple of hundred yards north of the Bathgate Junction on the Edinburgh-Glasgow (Queen Street) main railway line. At Newbridge the

M8 and M9 spin off to begin their courses to Greenock (through Glasgow) and Stirling respectively. It seems incredible that, even today, a motorway journey is not possible between Scotland's two biggest cities. Can you imagine London and Birmingham having no motorway connection between them? Indeed, the nearest motorway linking Scotland's capital with the south is the M6 at Carlisle!

Is it possible that Scottish passenger services in and out of Edinburgh's Waverley station are so good as to stifle public demand for superior motorway links?

Admittedly, a fast car journey is possible between the centres of Glasgow and Edinburgh in about 60min, provided the eastbound driver uses the new outer city bypass to avoid the Corstorphine traffic-jams. Here combined traffic from the M8 and M9 motorways have to filter along the narrow St John's Road, causing havoc to community life and local transport links. Ironically, the local rail terminus was sited only yards from this congestion centre; the Corstorphine branch closure is a puzzle still seeking an answer.

Despite the nearness of a motorway link, the 50min spent over a coffee and a newspaper in the Glasgow-Edinburgh train offer an attractive alternative to the inter-city traveller over a distance where rail could not normally expect to offer the road system a powerful challenge.

The same applies in the case of journeys between Edinburgh and Dundee. Although barely 50 miles apart on the map, the two cities are divided by the great firths of Forth and Tay with the Fife peninsula between them. While the Forth and Tay Road Bridges have removed the water-crossing problem (although tolls have to be paid), the Fife road-system is not worthy of the county, and motorists are apparently in the habit of driving between Edinburgh and Dundee via Perth, using the M90 south of that town and the dual-carriageway along the Tay Valley on the northern stretch. Even a Class 27 diesel and four coaches now replaced by Sprinter units on around an 80min schedule has offered a viable alternative, and serves a number of large Fife towns as well.

Interestingly, it is the Edinburgh-Inverness journey, through the beautiful but hardly well-populated Highlands, where road transport offers a serious challenge to rail. The motorist travelling from Edinburgh can take the M90 to Perth and then join the upgraded A9, making a journey time of 3½hr to the northern capital quite practicable. For the train to equal this, IC125 performance is required, and is now provided.

Perhaps the rather surprising competition offered the railways up the central spine of Scotland, with its sparse population, can be explained by the comparatively poor train service in the last few decades, suggesting that public dissatisfaction with rail services often results in corresponding road investment. Expresses to and from Euston, to say nothing of the Scottish cities, had to stop to pass other traffic in stations like Birnam and Carrbridge, or for locomotive purposes in steam days at Blair Atholl and Aviemore. A decision to single the line over Druimuachdar not long before the oil business exerted its importance in the North of Scotland, was typical of the shortsightedness of the powers-that-be. This singling increased the danger of unpunctuality and delay, and a second line had subsequently to be relaid. As a result there was a public demand for the old A9 road to be upgraded — and this has happened. The old Highland Railway line now has a powerful rival ribboning its way side by side with it through the mountains.

There seems to be less of a public outcry about the lack of motorway provision between Edinburgh and the other three Scottish cities, however, and this may be directly because the railway already offers a perfectly acceptable passenger service. This is a compliment to the way the old North British company conceived its services as — effectively — a northern extension of Anglo-Scottish expresses, allowing through journeys without changing trains.

The railway has saved Edinburgh from being defaced with urban flyovers and spaghetti-type junctions, despite having a comparable, if not a higher, percentage of car-owners than for example Glasgow, where the motorway reigns supreme.

Of course, the railway cannot solely claim credit from sparing Edinburgh the ravages of motorway predation. The city's Cockburn Association — one of the first civic amenity societies in the world — has always been active in this respect. Indeed one of the first targets of Lord Cockburn's wrath was in fact the railway itself! That eminent 19th century jurist and historian published a pamphlet in 1849 entitled *The Best Ways of Ruining the Beauties of Edinburgh*, arguing against the laying of tracks in Princes Street Gardens, although it was by then too late to stop the Edinburgh & Glasgow Railway doing so, and His Lordship was dead by more than 15 years when the contentious issue of doubling the tracks through the Gardens was raised. Looking back, it seems unarguable that having trains unobtrusively traversing Princes Street Gardens is better than, for example, a six-lane highway brutalising the Meadows area, as was proposed in the 1960s, and sensibly rejected.

Early developments

From the Bronze Age, Edinburgh owes its early origins to tribal settlements on the formerly volcanic hills of the area, giving defensive security to whoever controlled them on the southern shore of the Firth of Forth. Sited a few miles east of the lowest short crossing-point of the Forth estuary, the Edinburgh area soon adopted its now-traditional role as a route-centre, thanks to its rocky fastness in the midst of the fertile Lothians, straddling what became formalised paths between England and central Scotland. These included Dere Street, the main Roman road connecting the Tyne with the Forth nearly 1,800 years before the East Coast main line did so.

Below:
Empty coaching stock to form the 15.15 to Oban and Mallaig passes through Princes Street Gardens from Haymarket Depot in March 1990 and approaches Waverley station formed of Class 156 'Super Sprinters' Nos 156453/156450. *Brian Morrison*

As with ethnographic history, so with railways.
The railway confirmed the city's role as a route
centre, and Edinburgh's location on the edge of the
Lothian coalfield gave it added importance. It is no
surprise to find that Scotland's first authorised
waggonway — planned only two years after
England's first at Woolaton, Notts, in 1604 — was
probably built only 10 miles from Edinburgh at
Inveresk. Coal was the spur for such an early rail
development — at a time when Scotland and
England had newly become united under a single
monarch, and Shakespeare was still working on
Hamlet and *Macbeth*. This first Scottish railway was
the idea of Thomas Tulloch who had, according to
the records of the Privy Council of Scotland

'imployit the maist pairt of his youth in
uncuth nations in searching and learning
the knawledge for making and practizeing
of ingynis and workis for the commodious
and aisie transporting of coillis (coal)
betuix the colpotis, sey and salt panes of
this realm'.

Translated, this simply means that Tulloch, who had
returned to Scotland from a technical apprentice-
ship in England following his father's death, had
'employed the most part of his youth in foreign
nations in searching for, and learning, the technology for the making and running of constructions
and works for the commodious and easy transporting of coal between the mines, sea, and salt pans
of this realm'. (Salt pans were an important part of
the then Scottish economy, requiring coal for the
production of salt by boiling sea-water).

The Council went on to award Tulloch a patent for
his 'ingyne' (a machine or construction, not an
engine in the modern sense) to last his lifetime,
provided this was 'ane work and ingyne nocht
known in this kingdom at na time of before'. Thus we
know that the Edinburgh area could probably boast
a form of railway before most European capitals. No
vestiges of this early waggonway remain in the
Inveresk area, just to the south of Musselburgh, but
as they would have been wooden anyway, this is not
surprising.

However, a more lasting provenance exists for
Scotland's third railway — the second appears to
have been at Stacks near Bo'ness around 1646 — and
this third line was definitely built at Tranent in
1722. Again, this was a coal-fostered development
about 12 miles from Scotland's capital, and its
course is still visible to the naked eye, being crossed
several times a day by IC125s and IC225s. When the
clans were 'out' for the Old Pretender in 1715, the
local Earl of Winton backed the wrong side — the
Jacobites. Consequently his estate was sequestered
by the Crown, his mines in the Tranent area coming
under the administration of the progressive York
Buildings Company.

The result was a horse-drawn waggonway
designed to carry Tranent coal to the tiny port of
Cockenzie. The line achieved notoriety by becoming
the first to be fought over in a pitched battle,
Sir John Cope's Government troops fleeing from the

forces of Charles Edward Stewart over its track at the Battle of Prestonpans in 1745, during the Second Jacobite Rebellion.

A mere 70 years later, in the year of Waterloo, the single line of wooden rails — laid to what later became known as metre gauge — were replaced by those of cast iron. These in turn gave way to wrought-iron rails after alteration to standard gauge in the 1850s, the decade of the Crimean War, although the line appears to have been taken up by 1886. In 1939, while a new war darkened Europe, local historian George Dott discovered a few vestiges of track at Cockenzie and interviewed a fisherman who remembered breaking up the original wagons. Ironically, the East Lothian power station of Cockenzie is now a centre for modern MGR operation between there and the Lothian coalfield which inspired so much early waggonway development.

Nor was this the only evidence of Edinburgh's part in the pre-history of the British railway system. The late-lamented railway historian, John Thomas, has pointed out that the city's *Scotsman* newspaper was advocating such a rail network, powered by steam locomotives in 1824, even before Stephenson had exhibited its potential to the world. Not only that, but a perusal of some of the learned periodicals of the time — such as the *Transactions* of the Royal Scottish Society of Arts — shows considerable interest in railways among the city's intelligentsia.

Above:
Despite her Scottish name, *St Mungo* — the patron saint of Glasgow — 'A1' Pacific No 60145 was a Gateshead engine, and is seen here at Prestonpans in June 1952 on a down express conveying a Penzance-Aberdeen through coach. *Real Photos*

Pioneering railways

The early years of the Scottish railway system have been well-documented, particularly by John Thomas and C. J. A. Robertson (see Bibliography), so only a brief account is required here, and a graphic summary displayed in Table 1. Edinburgh saw its first station open in the St Leonard's district in 1831, and passenger traffic on the Edinburgh & Dalkeith Railway gradually developed during the next five years. The E&D was effectively a horse-drawn waggonway, not even constructed to standard gauge, but it established the importance of the Lothian coalfield and confirmed the practicality of passenger travel in the Lothians.

Three railways soon laid their tracks into the Scottish capital — the much-renamed Edinburgh Leith & Newhaven, with its Canal Street terminus at Waverley Bridge; the Edinburgh & Glasgow at Haymarket (later Waverley); and the North British, with its lines from what is now Waverley to Berwick-on-Tweed and Hawick. The last two

Table 1
Edinburgh's Railway and Canal Companies, c1830-1950

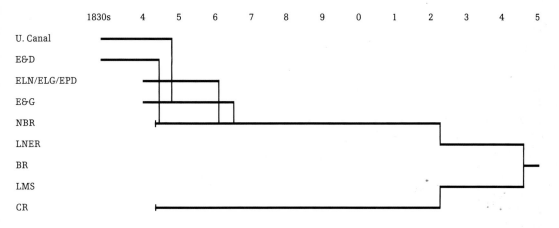

Key:

U. Canal = Union Canal, later to British Waterways Board (included to show history of railway ownership).

E&D = Edinburgh & Dalkeith.

ELN/ELG/EPD = Edinburgh Leith & Newhaven, later Edinburgh Leith & Granton, later Edinburgh Perth & Dundee.

E&G = Edinburgh & Glasgow.

NBR = North British Railway.

LNER = London North Eastern Railway.

BR = British Railways (later British Rail).

LMS = London Midland & Scottish Railway.

CR = Caledonian Railway.

companies were to have a seminal effect on Scottish railway development, their trackbeds still providing IC125s with pathways to north and south, while the North British, from its modest beginnings, became the biggest, if not the most prestigious, of Scotland's railways.

All three pioneering railways (as opposed to the non-standard gauge E&D) met at the present site of Waverley around 1846/7, establishing it as the capital's principal travel centre for the next century and a half at least. Waverley will receive detailed consideration in due course, while all the above-mentioned railways will be examined in chapters on their principal stations in the city, whether still in use, or, as in the case of St Leonards and Scotland Street, on their almost archaeological remains.

1
Edinburgh as a Rail Centre

Mention has already been made of Edinburgh's traditional role as a route centre, and for recent — and unfortunately negative — confirmation of this in a railway sense one needs only to analyse how a wrong transport decision made in 1970 has left its mark on the Anglo-Scottish transport network nowadays.

It was in 1970 that British Rail announced the extension of its West Coast electrification scheme from Weaver Junction, where the Liverpool lines leave the WCML, northwards to Glasgow. It was exciting then to anticipate the wires stretching over Shap and Beattock, and time brought no disappointment with the eventual spectacle of Class 86s and 87s powering effortlessly up and over these summits at speeds that steam-hauled trains could only aspire to going downhill.

But there was a disappointment for Edinburgh citizens in discovering that BR was unprepared — or unwilling — to extend the catenary to the Scottish capital. It seemed illogical to electrify the WCML north through Carlisle and Carstairs to Glasgow and then omit to include the Carstairs-Edinburgh section. It is, after all, less than 30 miles long and would have added to the electric rail network a population centre of some 400,000, one which is a major tourist attraction in July and August. This is to say nothing of an almost equal number of souls in Fife who have no direct rail access to the northern connections of the WCML, or the city of Dundee which hardly has a much better access route to the southwest.

It is almost as if the recent East Anglian electrification scheme from London's Liverpool Street through Colchester and Ipswich stopped short at, say, Diss instead of going on to Norwich. Why include Norwich when Ipswich has an electric service? Why electrify to Edinburgh when Glasgow is being served? There is no sensible answer to either riddle. Fortunately for the good people of Norwich, there was no question of their not receiving the benefits of electrification — but Scotland's capital was not so lucky.

The only plausible reason for not stretching the wires from Carstairs into Edinburgh was not likely to have been one of cost, but of labour relations. The newspapers at the time carried considerable speculation that any extension of the catenary into

Edinburgh from the west would prejudice the future of the Newcastle-Edinburgh section of the ECML. Union leaders appeared fearful that electrification would involve switching London-Edinburgh Inter-City services from East to West Coast routes, with existing ECML trains going no farther north than Newcastle, the route they presently followed being downgraded to single-line status, or perhaps lifted altogether.

These fears were perhaps understandable at the time, although they were ultimately nullified, firstly, by the success of the IC125 services on the ECML and, secondly, by the East Coast's strategic importance in relation to North Sea oil — something that should have been increasingly obvious very early in the 1970s. What a pity that the High Speed Train concept was not available a few years earlier! If their speed potential over long distances had been fully demonstrated — even if only in test runs on this line — before the electrification teams had finished in 1973/74, the 125s would have shown that services from King's Cross and Newcastle to Edinburgh had nothing to fear from the West in terms of speed. It would surely have been impossible to operate any Euston-Waverley service in less than the time being taken by the newly-electrified *Flying Scotsman*. A WCML service would have taken about 5hr, unless there had been considerable realignment of the difficult turnoff at Strawfrank Junction (Carstairs), which makes a bad preparation for the Cobbinshaw climb. While not a motive power problem for electrics, this would not exactly be an ideal ground on which to compete against IC125s.

Interestingly, at the time of the commissioning of the new Edinburgh signalling centre, BR revealed that 'immunisation' — usually the first step in the electrification of a line — had already taken place between Edinburgh and Midcalder Junction, well on the way to Carstairs, and this electrification was given the go-ahead in 1989 and completed in 1990.

In addition, there has always been scope to direct more Aberdeen-NW England/Midlands traffic from the WCML through Waverley, with the Granite City growing in importance in the last quarter of our century, thanks to its proximity to Britain's vital oil fields. In 1986 Brian Perren was writing in *Modern Railways* about the limitations of Glasgow as a destination for electric WCML trains, owing to its

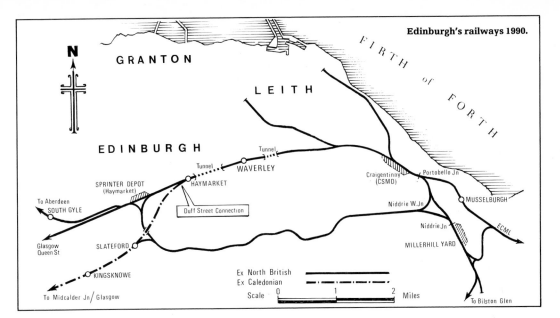

lack of a through station. The powerful rivalry of air services in and out of Glasgow Airport — which now enjoys international airport status — means that rail traffic to and from the north of Glasgow is increasingly necessary to balance the Inter-City ledgers in this area.

Services from the south to Aberdeen, Perth, or Inverness, have to avoid Scotland's largest city by turning off at Law Junction near Motherwell and switching from electric to diesel power before proceeding through Cumbernauld, Larbert, and Stirling northwards. Glasgow could be included in this itinerary if the railway authorities were prepared to run trains into Glasgow Central where they would have to reverse and then join the line at Rutherglen Junction to Coatbridge incurring an extra 15 miles or so, with doubled 'pathing' requirements in and out of one of Britain's busiest termini. An additional drawback is that 'under sector accounting procedures, part of the costs of the Rutherglen-Coatbridge line would be passed from the freight to the passenger business', points out Perren.

What all this illustrates — admittedly in a decidedly negative way — is Edinburgh's outstanding potential as a route centre. With electrification of the Carstairs-Edinburgh line, services from the Midlands and Lancashire to Aberdeen could be routed through Edinburgh instead of Law Junction, vastly increasing the trains' potential travelling public while the Law Junction line would still be available for Glasgow (Queen Street)-Aberdeen services on its section north of Greenhill (Lower) Junction. A change in motive power would still be required in Edinburgh for through Aberdeen trains from the WCML but this would hardly be time-

consuming, as reversal of direction is necessary; allowing simultaneous coupling and uncoupling at each end of the train.

To quote Perren again,

'In order to obviate the tedious transfer between Glasgow's Central and Queen Street stations, an increasing number of passengers travelling between the English Midlands and the North West and stations in Central and the north of Scotland are opting to go via Edinburgh.'

The impending electrification of the Carstairs-Edinburgh line brought new benefits for southbound travellers from Edinburgh with the introduction of the 1990 Summer timetable. For the first time there was no need for diesel-hauled trains from Edinburgh to sit at Carstairs waiting to join on to an electric-hauled train from Glasgow Central.

Changing trains at this Lanarkshire outpost was something of an Edinburgh folk-tradition. Most citizens can tell some horror story of changing trains there, and being sidelined in silent stationary coaching-stock while comfortable Glaswegians swept past on the WCML with no apparent motive power or coupling/uncoupling problems.

With the introduction of electric services to Edinburgh in 1991, Carstairs held the key to allow IC225 trains from King's Cross to Edinburgh to proceed to Glasgow Central.

One slight drawback of having electric trains approaching the city from West as well as East concerns Haymarket, whose station is a perennial puzzle to the uninitiated traveller. But more of that later. Let us first examine Waverley station — the heart of Midlothian's railways.

2
Waverley: The Heart of Midlothian's Railways

Although no longer the largest station in Great Britain, the Waverley is undoubtedly a major landmark at the heart of the city. Perhaps it is not the most conspicuous of landmarks, sunk as it is in the east-to-west valley between the Old and New Towns, spanned by North Bridge and Waverley Bridge, and hemmed in by the Calton Hill to the east and the Mound to the west.

The Waverley's somewhat abyssal situation has unfortunately nullified the advantages springing from its central urban position. Passengers have always found the climb up from the platforms to street-level to be unpleasantly strenuous to all but the supremely fit. For eight decades the local newspapers' columns have repeated the plea for escalators to be installed at the Waverley Steps up to Princes Street – but to no avail. To make matters worse, the NBR constructed its through suburban platforms on the *south* side of the station, as far away from the city's administrative centre, with its considerable potential for commuters, as it is possible to be within the station's premises.

It is sad but true, that most Edinburgh citizens never enter the Waverley station at all except as a starting and finishing point for their holiday journeys or to welcome friends visiting for the Festival. This probably accounts for the enormous fund of affection the capital's inhabitants feel towards their major railway station – a place to anticipate long-awaited vacations and to express pleasure at the sight of a well-loved acquaintance, but we'll get there by bus or car, thank you!

Before 1892

A station has been on this site since 1846. Here, the North British Railway built its east-facing terminus for traffic to Berwick and Hawick – in so doing sweeping away the city's Physic Garden, where plants of pharmaceutical value were grown, and causing the historic Trinity Church to be moved stone by stone to a new site – a relocation described by Lord Cockburn, the pioneering civic conservationist, as 'an outrage by sordid traders, virtually consented to by a tasteless city and sanctioned by an insensible parliament'.

The Edinburgh & Glasgow brought traffic into the General station (as it was then known) from the west from 1 August 1846, some six weeks after the NBR had begun operations there. Tucked away in the northwest corner of this complex was Canal Street station which opened on 17 May 1847, and will be described in due course.

So there were two (arguably, three) stations here between 1847 and approximately 1868, when the NBR made Canal Street redundant by constructing a new line to Granton and Leith through Abbeyhill. By 1854 the name 'General' had been superseded by that of 'Waverley', although the latter is not an

Left:
Waverley station, looking eastwards from the Scott Monument. The twin carriageway ramps are clearly visible entering the station at a gradient of 1 in 15 down from Waverley Bridge (in the foreground), while North Bridge can be seen striding across the huge expanse of glass roof. The Balmoral Hotel is on the left, with the new Waverley Centre, once the site of a proposed Caledonian station, nearer your intrepid cameraman.
Author

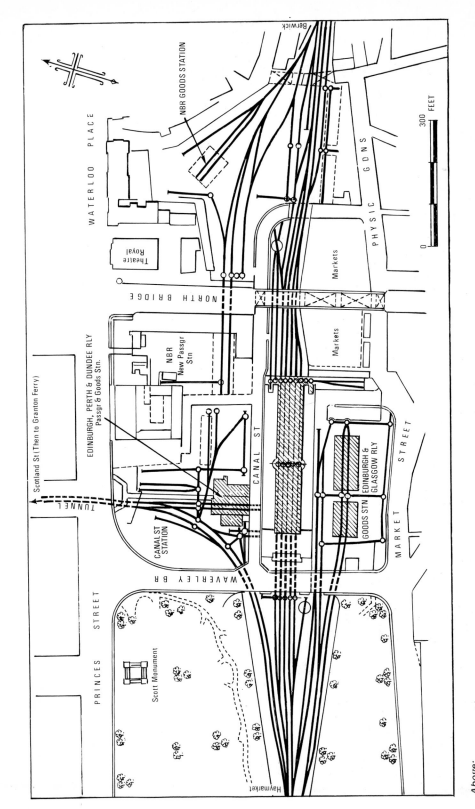

Above:
General and Canal Street stations 1860.

17

indigenous name, and owes its Scottish usage entirely to Edinburgh's own Wizard of the North, Sir Walter Scott. Not content with furnishing the North British with a name for its major Edinburgh station, its main line to Carlisle, and a host of NBR locomotives, Sir Walter's other posthumous contribution to railway history was to inspire the name of the LNER's first 'A4' Pacific, *Silver Link,* taken from his poem *The Lay of the Last Minstrel.*

At the time of the Joint station's opening, local author W. H. Lizars painted a word-picture of the new building which contrasts enormously with its subsequent appearance and character before rebuilding:

'Separate doors (in the Waverley Bridge building) lead, by easy and elegant flights of stairs to the platforms of the respective railways on the level of the line below. There are waiting apartments on the platform and . . . (a restaurant) where the wayfarer, if so disposed, may comfort his inner man with all manner of delicious condiments. The *coup d'oeil* of the platform station is considerable, its proportions faultless, and its lightness, elegance, and airiness, impart grace to its fine and finished vista . . . We do not know anything as yet to compare to this grand railway arcade, save the Great Central Railway Station at Derby . . .'

Above:
Compare this 1847 watercolour, accomplished from the the then-new Scott Monument, with the view in 1987. The painting by Joseph Ebsworth shows in the middle distance the newly-opened Canal Street terminus, with its double-track line to the Granton ferry proceeding under Princes Street by way of the Scotland Street tunnel. There was a spur line connecting the Edinburgh Leith and Granton tracks with the Edinburgh & Glasgow to the right (out of the picture). The longitudinal appearance of the Joint (later Waverley), with its two platforms, is visible, on the middle right of the painting, providing a remarkable contrast to the present-day sea of glass.
City of Edinburgh Museums and Art Galleries

As the 1860 plan shows, the original station had but two platforms, neither stretching beyond Waverley Bridge on the west side or even reaching North Bridge on the east. Additional terminal accommodation had to be extemporised northeast of the main train-shed, but space had also to be found on the site for no fewer than three goods stations. Some rationalisation was possible by the mid-1860s with both the Edinburgh Perth & Dundee and Edinburgh & Glasgow being absorbed by the North British, although Caledonian blue also appears to have been regularly seen at Waverley until the 1890s when that company's Princes Street terminus was finished at long last.

Subsequent writers have been less kind than Lizars about the pre-1890 station, with its later infamous reputation for scrambled timetables, harassed porters, and bewildered passengers. The reader is referred to the histories of the North British Railway written by C. Hamilton Ellis and the late John Thomas, for the point to be forcibly made. Both suggested that delays anywhere on the British rail system could often be accounted for by the confusion reigning at Waverley in the years before 1890. Ellis even argues fancifully but amusingly about a mythical round-the-world train being delayed, not at such remote outposts as Irkutsk or Medicine Hat, but at the old Waverley!

For a contemporary view of Waverley in the latter part of the 19th century, we can rely on the much-travelled railway expert W. M. Acworth, whose opinion still hits the reader's eye straight out of the pages of his book *The Railways of Scotland,* written in 1889:

'Edinburgh often boasts its superiority to
Glasgow. In one respect at least – its
railway stations – it must acknowledge its
vast and apparently hopeless inferiority.
The Caledonian station is a wooden
shanty. As for the North British, in its
original prospectus, dated August 1843, it
expressed the determination "to avoid all
useless expense in ornamental works at
stations or otherwise", and its worst
enemy will scarcely deny that it has kept
its promise . . . As for the Waverley, what
pen can do justice to it?'

One which tried belonged to another railway author of the time, or more correctly the joint pen of E. Foxwell and T. C. Farrer. Their slightly inaccurately-entitled book of 1889 *Express Trains, English and Foreign* (reprinted by Ian Allan Ltd, 1964) includes the following description of the platform scene at Waverley before the opening of the Forth Bridge.

'Trains of caravan length come in
portentously late from Perth, so that each
is mistaken for its successor; these have to
be broken up and remade in insufficient
sidings, while bewildered crowds of
tourists sway up and down amongst
bewildered porters on the narrow village
platform reserved for these most
important expresses . . .'

The description of 'narrow village platforms' provided for Anglo-Scottish expresses at the pre-1892 Waverley was probably no exaggeration. The Waverley Bridge had no fewer than 11 spans, compared to those of its present-day successor, and one of its abutments reduced the old main Up platform to being 'a mere ledge in a tunnel' as one

contemporary critic put it. Indeed, Thomas records that a tall man could straddle the 4ft width of such platforms. The prospect of a lengthy train drawn up beside such a narrow space, with porters and passengers struggling past open carriage doors and each other, must have resembled the last minutes of the *Titanic.*

Acworth presciently believed that the station would have to be extended into the Princes Street Gardens area, and speculated in 1889 as to what would happen if it did not:

'Unquestionably the gardens are beautiful,
and a railway station unlovely; but after
all, the Princes Street hotelkeepers and
shopkeepers would hardly wish to be left
in solitude to enjoy the spectacle. Next year
when the Forth Bridge will be open . . . how
would Edinburgh, with its metropolitan
dignity, like it, if next summer some of the
London expresses halted for half a moment
outside the town at Millerhill Junction,
contemptuously uncoupled a carriage or
two, and then ran on by the sub line direct
to the Forth Bridge?'

Accommodation problems at Waverley became impossibly acute after the opening of the Forth Bridge in 1890. This triggered a move by the North British to rebuild Waverley, an initiative complicated by attempts by the Caledonian to promote an underground line beneath the length of Princes Street to the Waverley Market area and then approach Leith via a tunnel through the Calton Hill. The NBR managed to see off this threat to its stronghold – by enlisting civic support for a shorter line to what became Leith Central – and lavished £1.5 million on rebuilding the Waverley station in the years 1892-97.

1892-1969

Empowered by an Act of Parliament dated 5 August 1891, the NBR created the biggest station in the kingdom – at least until Glasgow Central and London's Waterloo caught up a few years later.

It is in fact two termini back to back, effectively configured as a massive island platform with its outer faces capable of accommodating two full-length trains apiece. The 'suburban' platforms on the south side duplicate the island concept, giving a total at one time of no fewer than 21 platforms. The whole area covers 23 acres (half an acre bigger than London's Liverpool Street station at that time), and boasted nearly 14,000ft of platform length capable of accommodating 358 contemporary coaches simultaneously, signalled from four boxes.

The existing design of transverse-valley glazed roof was retained, supported by lattice girders

Above:
Waverley's impressive Booking Hall, swept away when the modern Travel Centre was built in time for the 1970 Commonwealth Games. Note the formidable wooden ticket office, the (now closed) passage in the right background leading to the eastern concourse, and the NBR crest, uniting the insignia of Edinburgh and Berwick-upon-Tweed, on the tiled floor.
Royal Commission Ancient Monuments, Scotland

Left:
Compare this view with that of the old Booking Hall, seen here in 1987 from broadly the same angle, looking towards the Food Court. *Author*

between cast-iron columns engineered by Hannah, Donald & Wilson. The local firm of Cunningham Blyth & Westland were the principal contractors, providing a central two-storey building, 'elaborately pilastered', as the Penguin *Buildings of Scotland* guide describes it, arranged around a central court area. This, as the accompanying illustration shows, incorporated a dignified booking hall, replete with varnished timber and looking capable of withstanding a siege of reasonable longevity, with its defenders rarely obliged to show themselves to the surrounding public. The hall was dignified by the NBR insignia embellished in each corner of the tiled floor and the western end of the court included a

seated statue of John Walker, the line's General Manager from 1874-90. At the opposite end was the War Memorial, now resited on an external wall of the building, facing Platforms 10/11. A passage, now closed to the public, led to the eastern platforms.

The modern powers-that-be decided to replace the central booking office with ticket, information, and reservation offices within an arcaded development on the south side of the court at the end of the 1960s. The west side holds modern Solari travel indicators for departures and arrivals, with the central court area cleared for passengers to view these easily. A restaurant complex now comprises much of the east, and part of the north, sides of the area, comprising what is known as a 'food court'. The Author would like to offer his opinion as to its equivalent of the 'delicious condiments' mentioned by Lizars — unfortunately on my last visit, the staff in one of the snack-bars were too busy talking to one another to make the slightest effort to serve the public. Doubtless an atypical event, but one major disadvantage of the court area seems to be the necessity to service it from road vehicles, causing not a little public inconvenience.

Retail shop units back on to Platform 1 opposite the northern side of the central building. These represent an attempt to provide a market-like atmosphere, but unfortunately seriously reduce the width of Platform 1, to an extent this author can only consider as inconvenient if not downright dangerous. Perhaps not capable of being straddled by a tall man, but frequently choked by waiting passengers often oblivious to the fast-approaching IC125 from either direction.

Platforms 10/11 on the south side of the main station are the site of a short-stay car park and a Pullman Lounge. The latter ministers to the immediate pre-journey needs of first-class rail travellers, providing refreshments and some office facilities, as well as meeting room accommodation.

From 1902 the Waverley has been topped by the adjacent North British Hotel, whose clock, traditionally 2min fast, is a major Scottish landmark in its 175ft tower. The hotel was designed by the Beattie brothers, and posed major construction problems when it was discovered that dynamiting the foundations – thought necessary because of the volcanic rock of the area – threatened to cause considerable damage to neighbouring properties. Eventually, the foundations had to be dug by hand, so it is no surprise that the building took over four years to complete. John Thomas records that the canny NBR arranged the wiring so that not more than one electric light could be turned on simultaneously in each bedroom!

The hotel's main entrance comprises the only street-level doorway on the south side of Princes Street before the Royal Scottish Academy on the Mound, and there is a lift-shaft between the hotel and station concourse. At one time the hotel's boilers were fuelled by coal supplied by railway wagons from a siding off the northernmost through line. The hotel was disposed of to commercial interests in the early 1980s and was due to reopen in 1991 following comprehensive refurbishment as the Balmoral Hotel, reflecting the name of its current owners – although Edinburgh citizens will no doubt continue to refer to 'the NB'.

Interestingly, the positioning of Edinburgh's major pre-1914 hotels, such as the North British, has suggested to one historian that, if considered with the comparative lack of hotel accommodation in the suburbs, Edinburgh was very much a 'transfer' destination in those times. At most, visitors would pay a brief visit to the city's central attractions, but did not intend to be far removed from the railway giving access to their next Scottish destination. Certainly, it was only the coming of the Motor Age –

specifically since 1945 – that has seen the growth of large hotels on the city boundaries.

Nowadays, the closure of the Waverley Route and of most intermediate stations to Berwick-on-Tweed, as well as all southeast Scotland's passenger branch termini with the exception of North Berwick, has greatly lessened the demand for platform capacity on the east side of the station. Platforms 2 to 6 inclusive, along with 8 and 9, have vanished from the destination board – which has itself disappeared from the eastern concourse. The area of platforms 3 to 6 has now been taken over at the station end by a Post Office installation and a BR operations depot, the latter – booking-on point for 250 footplate staff – graced by an impressive Pilkington glass wall facing the track at Platform 7. This is the only terminal arrival/departure point on this side of the station and 7's bufferstops are the site of the first, symbolic, emplacement of a catenary mast, as part of the ECML electrification in Scotland. Erected in the spring of 1985, the column has a plaque announcing that it is the first of 33,000 such masts north of the Border. Platforms 8 and 9 have given way to a car park, their tracks greatly truncated to form loading points for Motorail car traffic at the east end.

Number 9 was the traditional departure point for the 'Waverley' express on its near-10hr journey to London St Pancras, it being a common sight on summer mornings in the years up to 1961 to see three magnificent Pacifics ready to leave Londonwards, with the 'Elizabethan' in the charge of an immaculate 'A4' (Haymarket and King's Cross engines on alternate days) from 10, a Carlisle Canal 'A3' at the next platform-edge on the 'Waverley' from 9, while over on the north side a Gateshead 'A1' would be readying itself to head the 'Flying Scotsman' from number 1. Great days!

Goods traffic was withdrawn from the Waverley area – the goods station being southeast of the station, at New Street – from the end of 1966. Today a large car park stretches towards New Street.

Signalling

Colour-light signalling was introduced to the Waverley as early as the mid-1930s, being modernised some 40 years later. The colour lights had themselves replaced a forest of semaphores, controlled by four signalboxes, one of which (at the eastern end) boasted what was at one time the longest continuous lever-frame (of 260 levers) on Britain's railways. Two of the smaller boxes, situated high against the retaining wall inside the overall roof, lasted another half-century into the 1980s. These had been utilised as station-announcer's offices after the installation of colour lights. Their former location inside the station's walls can only just be discerned immediately to the right of an arriving passenger descending the

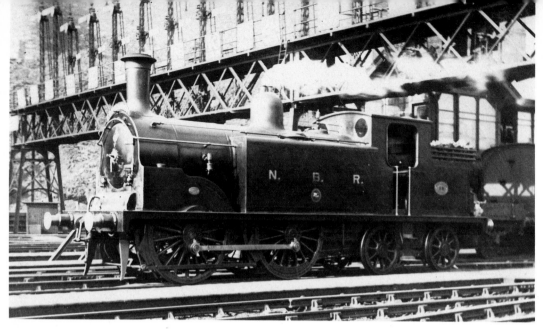

Posing beneath an impressive array of semaphore signals at Waverley's east end, Holmes NBR 'P' class 0-4-4T No 90 awaits her next tour of duty, probably on a North Berwick local, around the time of World War 1. She later operated on Border lines out of St Boswells before being withdrawn as LNER 'G7' No 9090 in September 1926. *Real Photos*

Waverley Steps, or to the right of one arriving from the Market Street entrance, after passing platforms 20/21.

The 1930s resignalling instituted two new boxes, at the east and west ends of the station. The latter still stands empty, close to the Mound south tunnel bore. When opened late in 1936, with 205 miniature levers, its Siemens equipment replaced double that number of manual levers in five mechanical boxes as far as Haymarket station. The eastern cabin has now been demolished, its 207 miniature levers going the same way as the manual frames they replaced in boxes at Waverley and at Abbeyhill Junction in November 1938.

The earlier modernisation of colour-light signalling was an impressive exercise for its time. This involved installing four-aspect signals, along with 15in diameter ground signals, and no fewer than 162 power-operated points. The system included power-operated roller-blind indicators to advise engine crews of their allocated platform, the numbers being painted white on black. Track-circuiting was introduced in 195 individual sections, a charge of 110V being fed along each rail; power was taken from the then Edinburgh Corporation public supply, with a 38hp four-cylinder engine standing by for emergency use.

Nowadays Waverley's signals stretch farther out than Abbeyhill and Haymarket! Opened in 1976, the new power box, situated on the site of the former goods yard to the south of the station, backing on to Market Street, controls over 220 routes miles. It is one of seven boxes covering the entire ECML, its range extending south to Tweedmouth and north to Cupar in Fife. Its other extremities are Newburgh, Oakley and Longannet north of the Forth, and Linlithgow, Bathgate, and West Calder in the west, at the time of writing.

Costing no less than £37 million, the new Centre controls nearly 600 main signals, over 200 position light signals, 472 point sets, and well over 1,400 track circuits. Its spider-like control of the area network is fringed by 28 relay rooms, some of which have local control panels which can be used for any localised emergency operations. Waverley's train announcers share console panels with the Centre's operators, allowing the former to communicate absolutely up-to-the-minute traffic information to station users.

Station facilities

As with signalling, so with station facilities; ScotRail invested £5.5 million in upgrading the Waverley in the years 1982-86. The new Travel Centre has already been mentioned, along with the Food Court, Operations Depot, and Pullman Lounge. Less noticeably than the piped Muzak and the airline-style 'hostesses' in their polythene 'bubble' on the western concourse, the Waverley also features a new parcels centre. This £0.25 million Red Star parcels depot now nestles under the northernmost carriageway, between platforms 17 and 19, featuring a conveyor system, closed-circuit TV, storage area and a security compound.

Above:
Diesel shunter No 08720 passes the Waverley West signalbox in 1976 with a parcels train for Haymarket. It is about to enter the Mound tunnel. *Brian Morrison*

Right:
Waverley West signalbox interior as photographed in the late 1970s, shortly before its duties were taken over by the present Signalling Centre a couple of hundred yards to the east.
Royal Commission Ancient Monuments, Scotland

Below right:
Until recently the Waverley Parcels Office, this former NBR building on Waverley Bridge, between the twin carriageways, is now a cafe/bar. It occupies the site of the first ticket office for the NB and Edinburgh & Glasgow railways before the station's first major rebuilding in 1892. *Author*

This has rendered redundant the Waverley Bridge office – since November 1984 – which fulfilled this function since the 1890s. It is now a privately-owned cafe-bar and sits on Waverley Bridge, between the openings of the two 1 in 15 gradient carriageways down to the station concourse. (One of the wing exteriors of the original booking office described earlier by Lizars still exists a few yards south on Waverley Bridge, forming the façade of part of the city's transport and tourist information centre.)

What of the future? Electric traction made its debut at the Waverley early in 1991 when the Carstairs-Waverley link was brought into use for through trains from the Midlands and the North-West.

In early summer the IC225 service started between Waverley and King's Cross, completing the ECML

electrification – or maybe not, if the Aberdeen lobby has its way.

The arrival of electric overhead wires in Waverley has not affected the station's appearance. Waverley is not a listed building, but is situated in a sensitive conservation area. The ECML electrification project managers were anxious to make the catenary as unobtrusive as possible in the station, and this they appear to have done, in the same way as discreet installations were required on the Royal Border Bridge at Berwick-on-Tweed.

There are longer-term plans for the 'Waverley valley', the continuation eastwards of Princes Street Gardens, which would reduce the visual impact of the station roof on one of the best-known views in Europe. Early plans included improvements to the layout and facilities of the station itself, and it is hoped that the final work will give Lord Cockburn's ghost no cause for concern!

Streamlining Waverley

The Waverley was one of the nation's earliest 'open' stations, so younger rail enthusiasts may be unfamiliar with the concept of platform tickets. Their older counterparts found themselves faced with a machine issuing platform tickets in 1938. It cost 3d (about 1.5p) to gain entry to the Waverley's platforms, and the machine generously offered change of sixpence or a shilling. In fact, it may have done business with casual visitors only — regular 'spotters' save a halfpenny by buying a 2½d (1p) return ticket to Abbeyhill or Piershill! At least the machine was sited in the correct station; platform tickets issued at Carlisle Citadel station in 1938 admitted the purchaser to Glasgow St Enoch!

In 1981 BR attempted to streamline the station's image by doing away with the 'Waverley' part of the station's soubriquet, and leaving it as 'Edinburgh' station pure and simple. Great was the wrath of public opinion against such a sacrilegious idea, a 5,000-name petition being collected in only four days by a local shopkeeper, and Waverley the station stayed. It was originally named to honour the novels of Sir Water Scott, who borrowed the title from Waverley Abbey in Surrey. That an English place-name has become such an indivisible part of Edinburgh heritage is a confirmation of the station's place in the city's life.

Services, past and present

'Waverley is . . . the major interface for Anglo-Scottish passenger traffic and thus the obvious focal point for BIT.'

BIT is Basic Interval Timetable in modern rail jargon, and as Brian Perren's words, quoted above, indicate, Waverley is the ideal centre for planning a cross-Border passenger service.

Its basis was the IC125 network from Dundee, Aberdeen, Glasgow to London (King's Cross) through Edinburgh, giving an hourly departure from Waverley southwards at 35min past the hour every hour from 07.35 to 18.35. (See Table 2.) In the reverse direction, by 1984 there were six IC125s daily between King's Cross and Waverley only, in addition to seven more serving Edinburgh on the way farther north.

Table 2
BIT: Edinburgh Waverley 1990

(Ignores isolated anomalies in frequency)

30min frequency	60min	Min/Hr	Comments
Glasgow (Q St)		00 & 30	
Dunblane		12 & 42	
Kirkcaldy		25 & 45	
	Cowdenbeath	15	
	Dundee	25	Not inc Aberdeen deps
	West Calder	20	
	London (KX)	00 or 30	17 services in 11 hours
	Bathgate	06	
	North Berwick	33	

The timetable presently in operation at Waverley at the time of writing is the product of transition. Gone is the precise gearing of internal Scottish services to the arrival and departure of IC125s on the King's Cross run, although the range of destinations available from Waverley is undiminished — the above table does not include nine Aberdeen departures, five of them at 40 minutes past the hour.

Table 3
Nos of Waverley departures arranged by destination distance 1910 and 1985

		(EASTBOUND)			
Miles	−15	15-30	30-60	60+	Total
1910	140[1]	8[2]	15[3]	16	179
1985	0	11	0	20	31
		(WESTBOUND)			
1910	46	0	38	23	107
1985	0[4]	43	97	30	164

1 Services to (in increasing order of distance); Leith Central, Joppa, North Leith, Granton, Musselburgh, Dalkeith, Polton, Gorebridge, Penicuik, Glencorse, Macmerry.
2 To Haddington, Gifford, North Berwick, Peebles, Dunbar.
3 To St Boswells, Galashiels (via Peebles), Hawick, Berwick.
4 Excludes North Berwick and Dunbar services travelling through Waverley and terminating at Haymarket.

Distances taken to nearest half-mile.

1910 trains which 'split' into two quite separate trains at a station on route after leaving Waverley are considered as two departures. Suburban Circle trains are included as westbound departures as they did not travel direct eastbound from Waverley at that time, but from Leith Central.

Examining traffic statistics of departures from Waverley over a 75-year period offers interesting reading. If one divides up outward travel into destinations of less than 15 miles, between 15 and 30, 30 and 60, and greater than 60, it is possible to assess whether Waverley, Scotland's highest-earning station, has altered its role in the national and local traffic pattern. The following list of train departures tabulated in Table 3 shows that it definitely has.

As can be seen immediately from Table 3, Edinburgh has maintained its services west and northwards in admirable style, in contrast to the depleted departure programme from the east end of Waverley. This is partly due to the addition to the westbound table of former Caledonian services on the Carstairs/Carlisle line and to Glasgow (Central), although even without considering these former Princes Street services there is still a net gain in 1985 departures over those of 1910 — 132 as against 107, an increase of nearly 25%. This is undoubtedly because modern motive power, with its potential for more intensive utilisation, has allowed ScotRail to offer a satisfactory regular-interval timetable. Admittedly, the Edwardian destination-board at Waverley would have shown far more intermediate stopping destinations than its present-day dot matrix electronic counterpart can, as will be examined later.

In contrast, even on a swift appraisal of Table 3, it is highly obvious that the eastbound passenger services from Edinburgh Waverley are a mere shadow of what they were in Edward VII's last year — in fact some 31 departures compared to nearly 180. This is only approximately 17% of the rail service offered to the citizens of southeast Scotland 75 years ago. Indeed, this discrepancy would have been worse had the old NBR not insisted on its Outer Circle passengers from Waverley (ie those wishing to reach Duddingston & Craigmillar) having to catch any available eastbound service to Portobello, and there change to a service out of Leith Central via Piershill. As a result, the only Suburban Circle departures listed in 1910 are for those westbound, meaning that the numerical difference between eastbound departure figures for 1910 and 1985 is artificially reduced.

Yet the Waverley's surviving long-distance services are undeniably improvements on their respective predecessors. Despite the fact that there are fewer Edinburgh-London expresses than in the summer of 1910, (when there were no fewer than 19, over the three major routes from Waverley and Princes Street), it is unarguable that the regular-

Left:
Passers-by watch from the walkway leading to the Waverley Steps, as 'A2' Pacific No 60529 *Pearl Diver* arrives with the 09.50 from Aberdeen in July 1953. *Brian Morrison*

Below:
An earlier generation of DMU sits in Waverley in May 1988 awaiting passengers for the 22.15 service for Dunblane. The train is formed of a 3-car BR Derby Class 108, with DMBS No 51936 leading. *Brian Morrison*

Below left:
Evening at Waverley in May 1988, and 150/2 class 'Sprinter' No 150257 awaits its departure time on the 22.20 service for Dundee. *Brian Morrison*

Bottom:
A late evening arrival at Waverley — IC125 power car No 43116 *City of Kingston-upon-Hull* sits in 'suburban' platform 21 at the head of the 17.00 ex King's Cross. *Brian Morrison*

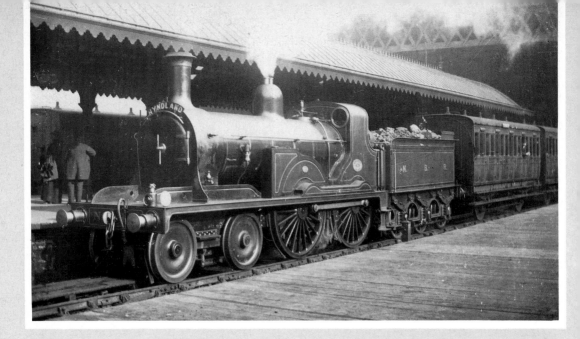

Above left:
Evoking a superb historical aura, Wheatley 4-4-0 No 420 stands at the west end of Waverley in 1897 with a Hyndland stopping train via Bathgate and Glasgow (Queen Street Low Level). This class, complete with 3¼ft diameter bogie wheels with 'solid centres of Bochum cast steel, giving to the engines a highly steam-rollerly appearance', according to C. Hamilton Ellis, were rebuilt by Holmes, and survived until World War 1. *Real Photos*

Left:
LNER No 9875 *Midlothian*, **one of the impressive North British Atlantics, sits at the west end of Waverley in 1938, probably at the head of an Aberdeen express.**
N. E. Stead collection

Top:
LNER Class K4 2-6-0 No 61993 *Loch Long* **heads out of Waverley with the Saturdays-only 17.20 to Dundee in July 1959.** *G. M. Staddon/N. E. Stead collection*

Above:
'Hush hush' on the 'Flying Scotsman'. Gresley's 'W1' 4-6-4 No 10000 leaves the east end of Waverley with the 10.00 departure for King's Cross one morning in 1930. The locomotive was paired with a corridor tender and on two occasions is believed to have worked the train non-stop over the 393 miles, the only non-Pacific to have done so.
Royal Commission Ancient Monuments, Scotland

Top:
Renamed 'The Elizabethan' in Coronation year, the non-stop 09.45 express to King's Cross pulls out of Waverley in July 1953, headed by Haymarket-based Gresley 'A4' Pacific No 60004 *William Whitelaw.*
Brian Morrison

Above:
The Gresley Class V1 and V3 2-6-2Ts were familiar for many years on Edinburgh suburban services, and this July 1953 scene shows St Margaret's-based 'V1' No 67659 arriving at Waverley with the 08.16 from North Berwick. *Brian Morrison*

Top:
The Midlothian town of Penicuik has grown three times over in population terms in this century, during which time it lost its passenger rail service. This was withdrawn in 1951, hampered by the roundabout route its trains took to reach Waverley via Eskbank. In this August 1964 picture 'J36' No 65234 reverses round its train, an enthusiasts' special, at the terminus.
Real Photos

Above:
Former Great Eastern 'F4' 2-4-2 tank No 7176 powers a Gifford-Waverley local out of Portobello station in 1931, shortly before the withdrawal of the service. This locomotive was later cascaded further north to the GNSR area. *Real Photos*

Right:
Towards the end of the Deltic domination of ECML expresses, No 55003 *Meld* makes a noisy and smoky exit from Waverley on the 16.00 to King's Cross in June 1977. To the left, No 47432 sits with a two-coach engineering train. *Brian Morrison*

With the drawbar gear wrapped in plastic to avoid icing up, the 08.45 Edinburgh to Edinburgh train via Cowdenbeath and Dunfermline, departs Waverley through the Mound tunnel in December 1989 formed of Strathclyde-liveried Class 156 'Super Sprinter' No 156510. Note the overhead in position for the Edinburgh-Carstairs electrification, and the portico of the National Gallery of Scotland above. *Brian Morrison*

Top:
Unusually pictured on a passenger train — probably a Sunday School special, judging by the excited passengers at the windows — 'J35' 0-6-0 No 9850 (later BR 64462) waits to leave Loanhead on the Glencorse branch in 1937. Passenger services had been withdrawn on the line four years earlier but until recently the line was still busy with MGR traffic between Bilston Glen and Cockenzie (or more occasionally Longannet).
Real Photos

Above:
For a number of years the Waverley-Glasgow Queen Street service was operated by Swindon-built express DMUs; one is seen about to leave Waverley in 1962. These units were replaced by the first generation of push-pull for the busy Glasgow service. *M. Mensing*

interval Edinburgh-London (King's Cross) service is a vast improvement in terms of speed and convenience. London-Edinburgh journey times were nearing the 4¼hr mark even before electrification. In contrast, even as late as 1932 steam-hauled expresses were constrained by the 8¼hr journey minimum agreed between the East and West Coast companies four years before the end of the last century, and steam's best scheduled time was 6hr.

But eastbound, Waverley is serving virtually nothing of its neighbouring area within 15 miles. Is Waverley's failure to communicate with its own hinterland not simply a result of road competition, inevitable in the present time? In fact, we have already seen that there has been less road investment in the Lothian road network than is the case elsewhere, so it becomes necessary to compare Waverley with another major station to see if its isolation from its own environs is typical. Table 4 directly compares Edinburgh's station with Glasgow's larger terminus, and again, 1910 and 1985 figures are featured.

Table 4
Number of stations directly serviced within 15 route-miles Edinburgh (Waverley) and Glasgow (Central), 1910 and 1985

| | Edinburgh (Waverley) | | Glasgow (Central) |
	Eastbound	Westbound	(High & Low Levels)
1910	46	19	79
1985	3	12[1]	61[2]

1 Includes stations on former Caledonian line to Midcalder Junction.
2 Includes former GSWR stations (1985 figures).

Table 4 compares the number of modern destinations directly accessible within 15 route-miles of Waverley, with those of the station's 1910 services, as well as those of Glasgow Central traffic both in 1910 and in 1985. The latter station has been unfavourably compared to Waverley for its rigid terminal configuration, but there is no doubt that, with its reopened Low Level services, it still provides Glaswegians with an enviable local transport option. Not only that, but Waverley compares particularly badly *because* of its through capacity. Given the potential cost and inconvenience of short workings, there was all the more reason to prolong the life of such services as Corstorphine-North Berwick passing through Waverley.

In contrast, Glasgow Central — so unfavourably compared to Waverley hitherto — has maintained an admirable network of short-travel services. East Kilbride, Neilston, the Cathcart Circle stations, and Motherwell (to and from Central Low Level) are

within a 15 route-mile radius, with electric traction making an invaluable contribution to the modern transport scene. Perhaps it is no coincidence that the passenger emerging from the Central station finds him, or herself, as conveniently placed in the heart of the city as one could possibly wish — and no heart-stopping stairs or ramps to climb!

But the withdrawal of Edinburgh's short-distance trains is a real loss, and not an entirely easy one to understand. For example, North Berwick benefits from a regular fast service — yet curiously, the increase in the town's population has not been exceptional in comparative terms, nor is there any noticeable rise in its (deserved) summer popularity as a holiday resort to justify the survival of its rail service. This is in contrast to the increasing importance of say, Haddington, Penicuik, or Dalkeith in the postwar era of urban overspill reallocation.

Table 5 examines five Lothian towns which could reasonably be defined as 'satellites' of Edinburgh, and compares their past and present population figures. For this last information, the author is indebted to the Registrar General for Scotland.

Table 5
Waverley services to and from five principal Lothian communities

| | Distance from Waverley (miles) | Population* | | Increase % | Remarks |
		1911	1981		
North Berwick	22	3.2	5.1	59	Rail-served
Haddington	18	4.1	8.1	97	Stn cl 1949
Penicuik†	15	4.1	17.6	329	1951
Dalkeith	9	7.0	11.2	60	1942
Musselburgh	6	15.9	19.0	19	1964

* To nearest 1,000 † With Glencorse

The interesting conclusion to be drawn from the above table is, that major increases of populations in Edinburgh's satellite communities have not resulted in their retaining a rail service. Indeed, compared to North Berwick, all the above towns apart from Musselburgh have a larger population growth factor, and the latter had a substantially larger population in the first place. Otherwise, no pattern is apparent in this comparison, other than an increased likelihood of a branch terminus keeping its services the farther away it is from Waverley, and an apparently passive acceptance by the railway planners that these nearer traffic sources are lost to the network.

Perhaps the reason for this lies in operational expediency. North Berwick's compact one-line station — a sad contrast to what it once was, complete with hanging baskets of flowers on its two platforms — offers ScotRail a suitable eastern terminal point off the ECML for DMUs. The only alternative might be Dunbar, but the latter is obviously subject to any operational problems which can afflict the ECML, so North Berwick has benefited more than it might otherwise deserve to. A further bonus for the townspeople will be electrification. Preliminary approval was granted in 1990 by BR's London-based investment panel for a £1.3 million scheme. New trains would cost a further £7 million, and through electric running from North Berwick to West Calder via Waverley was mooted.

North Berwick's station is well-situated for its townspeople's convenience, more than, say, Musselburgh's was, but no more so than Dalkeith's terminus. This last-mentioned closed during World War 2, which is unfortunate, as a DMU service could have produced interesting results, and would have added at least some additional revenue to the Waverley Route's accounts. Interestingly, it was obvious during the lead-up to bus deregulation in the autumn of 1986 that both Musselburgh and Dalkeith were regarded by would-be operators as highly lucrative destinations, both now being additionally served by the formerly city-owned Lothian Region Transport buses.

Haddington's station was some half a mile from the town-centre, and the town's siting on the A1 has guaranteed a fast road journey into the city, although the Musselburgh bottleneck (now by-passed) was something of a problem.

Penicuik (pronounced 'Pennycook') is an interesting case. Having lost one of its major industries — papermaking — progressively over the years, the town has developed a suburban dormitory area to the north. Potential commuter traffic from here to Edinburgh has always found the road system simply too convenient to allow for any alternative, but interestingly, the northern part of this catchment area has almost absorbed the site of another former NBR terminus — Glencorse. Yet, as the above table demonstrates, the area's population growth has been spectacular, placing it well ahead of North Berwick.

It will be interesting to see if future local services to destinations west of the city become so intensive as to encourage DMU (or EMU) workings east of Waverley as an operational counterbalance. The huge municipal housing area of Wester Hailes — an area some five miles west of Princes Street, with a population big enough to equal most of Scotland's New Towns — had no rail service until May 1987, when a station was opened on the Waverley-Glasgow (Central) via Shotts line.

Will ScotRail utilise Waverley's potential for through passenger traffic? Would a Bathgate-North Berwick service not be a possibility? Perhaps Wester Hailes-Dalkeith? A recent (unofficial) survey of Dalkeith's future transport prospects was optimistic about the reopening of a rail link with Edinburgh, particularly since the tracks are barely two miles from the town, at Millerhill, although a bridge under the new bypass would be necessary. Unfortunately, Dalkeith's rail terminus, on its highly-convenient site, is lost forever to buses, whose challenge, the rail-minded observer cannot help reflecting, was capitulated to without much of a fight from the rail industry's powers-that-be.

At the time of writing the Bilston branch is still extant, running through the centre of Loanhead and with a former station at Gilmerton — would this be a suitable candidate for reopening to passenger traffic if the government's investment regulations were relaxed? Ironically, Gilmerton is now envisaged by Lothian Region as a Metro terminus, much to the chagrin of some of the local inhabitants.

The massive loss of Leith services (all vanished from Waverley's platforms by 1952) was probably inevitable once the city's Corporation tramways came into their own between the wars. The railway authorities need not argue that they were taken by surprise at the decline in the popularity of what was, in terms of actual journey time, an unbeatable service. As early as 1925 a local newspaper carried an editorial lambasting the LNER for not providing a series of escalators to Princes Street from the Waverley's platforms, and accurately predicting that this lack would mean the closure of many more suburban stations. Significantly, Princes Street Station, with its easier access/egress for pedestrians, held on to its Leith services for 10 years longer than Waverley, but their transfer to Waverley via the Duff Street connection would have been impossible without reversal at Slateford.

ScotRail conducted a survey of possible escalator provision in 1979, but without apparent result. An escalator would mean that it would no longer be possible to witness an endless queue for taxis on one of the (not-infrequent) days when road access to the station is cut off by street closures in connection with Festival, or other, processions. These cavalcades often assemble in Waverley Bridge and Market Street before proceeding along Princes Street, having effectively 'marooned' Waverley for some time. The author has seen this happen on the eve of the Festival, at the height of the tourist season, a time when Waverley has masses of visitors. It is apparently not BR's policy to object to these street closures, but one is tempted to wonder — why not?

In concluding this brief survey of ScotRail's BIT, and the manner in which Waverley provides an ideal base for it, one can only assume that the station's topography has benefited the long-distance inter-city traveller more than the local population. As long ago as the middle of the 19th century Edinburgh's Lord Provost Adam Black was quoted (with disapproval) by Lord Cockburn as remarking that Princes Street Gardens, the former bed of the then comparatively newly-drained Nor' Loch, was an ideal site for a railway to pass through the centre of Edinburgh. This is as true now as when it was then, but the failure to provide escalators — or any other kind of pedestrian access or egress aids — has nullified the station's local appeal. Is it a coincidence therefore that Waverley fails to provide any kind of transport link with such important regional centres as Haddington, Dalkeith, or Penicuik, all of which have greatly-increased populations as well as (at one time) reasonably central station sites?

Lothian people's loss would, it appears, be Britain's gain. It seems that, generally speaking, Waverley is not a viable passenger destination unless you are travelling more than 20 miles into, or out of it. This does not apply to Fife communities such as Inverkeithing or North Queensferry, which supply substantial numbers of commuters to and fro-ing across the Forth. As long as the Forth Road Bridge imposes tolls on traffic, many potential motorists will continue to use the train, if only, it seems possible, on principle as a protest against this anachronistic practice. On the other hand, the chronic congestion that greets motorists at the Barnton roundabout each morning must work in favour of the rail services — however crowded they have become. Edinburgh's comparative lack of on-street (and, indeed, off-street) parking places is obviously also a factor in this equation — one of less relevance to the Lothian towns, with their substantial areas of council housing, and heavy usage of bus services.

Transport historian D. L. G. Hunter has chronicled the rise of the Edinburgh-based Scottish Motor Traction Company, which began operations as early as 1906 and quickly established a reputation for reliable, cheap, and convenient public travel. As soon as legislation permitted them to do so, the LNER and LMS each bought a 25% interest in the company in 1929, and it is no surprise to find that there were no fewer than six branch-line closures in southeast Scotland within the next four years. (See Table 6.) In considering why SMT made their meteoric rise to success, one can only conclude that, again, Waverley's abysmal position may have had something to do with it.

While nothing continues to be done about the Waverley's atrocious pedestrian accessibility, it appears that BR, like the NBR and LNER before them, accept this unsatisfactory state of affairs. But Edinburgh's failure to maintain rail links with important satellite centres is a black mark against its record as an important route nucleus.

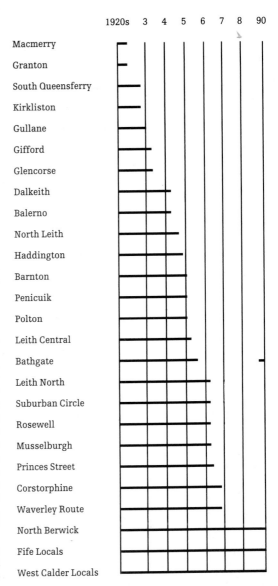

Table 6
Edinburgh Area Rail Closures & Surviving Services, 1920-90

Ignores temporary closure of the Dalkeith, Granton, and North Leith branches as an economy measure between 1917 and 1919.

3
West of Waverley

Railways in the park

Some public parks have a miniature railway to amuse visitors, but Edinburgh's most centrally-situated park, Princes Street Gardens, can go one better; for 140 years it has provided the park visitor with a real-sized railway entertainment. Between the Mound and Haymarket tunnels lay a quarter-mile of main line bridged by two footbridges and one limited weight road bridge. The last-named caused a local crisis in 1986 when a 14-ton mobile crane gained access to the area north of the bridge, despite its nominal 11-ton weight limit, and BR not unreasonably refused it permission to return the same way. In the end, the city's inhabitants and visitors were entertained to the sight of the crane being lifted out bodily over the railings into Princes Street by an even bigger version of itself!

Once there were two footbridges offering a different kind of spectacle — a never-ending railway cavalcade. This includes IC125s running between King's Cross and northern destinations, regular Class 158 services to and from Glasgow (Queen Street), and WCML trains to and from Carstairs Junction — with their associated light-engine movements between

Waverley and Haymarket depot — as well as DMU services to and from Fife, Dunblane, the Glasgow (Central) line, and Bathgate. A surprising amount of freight also passes through, possibly Aberdeen/Fife-Millerhill traffic avoiding crossing over the Glasgow/Bathgate/Stirling lines at Haymarket West.

The electrification to Carstairs has made necessary the removal of these bridges and their replacement with one high sided structure. Many mourned the passing of the lattice footbridges, on which many a railway enthusiast, including this author, first glimpsed a world of hot-breathing machines with romantic names like *Jingling Geordie*, *Laird of Balmawhapple*, and *Golden Plover*.

One Scottish transport historian has put forward the, on the face of it, surprising theory, that

Below:
Still adorned in its BR blue livery, which it lost in June 1952, Haymarket 'A4' Pacific No 60027 *Merlin* heads westwards through Princes Street Gardens with a Glasgow express. This locomotive received the unwanted attentions of Luftwaffe aircraft when working an East Coast train during wartime, but survived unscathed. *Real Photos*

Edinburgh has a larger community of railway enthusiasts than its more populous neighbour-city, Glasgow. But with Edinburgh parading its trains through its most famous park, much to the delight of generation after generation of city children, who is to say he is wrong?

Three decades ago, the prestigious American *National Geographic* magazine included an article on Scotland and the Scots. In its mandatory photograph of Edinburgh Castle seen from Princes Street Gardens, the brooding bulk of the battlements was seen apparently high above a cloud. The caption hastened to explain however, that the obtrusive vapour emanated from 'a passing loco'. It was not explained what it was doing in the middle of one of Scotland's most popular beauty-spots, nor have Edinburgh citizens ever felt it necessary to ask this same question.

The 'Caley': Princes Street station

Only a mile from Waverley are the few remains of Scotland's biggest closed station. The Caledonian Railway terminus was named after the city's most famous street, although it stood a few yards from the West End, and was actually situated in Rutland Street.

Opened in 1894, the terminus, which was always known to citizens as the 'Caley', was crowned by the prestigious Caledonian Hotel built above it and opened in 1903. The hotel still retains a major place in city life, having outlasted its 'parent' station since the latter's closure in September 1965. Interestingly,

Top:
'Shire' class 4-4-0 No 62733 *Northumberland* **heads a train from Fife through Princes Street Gardens in May 1958. The church in the centre background is St Cuthbert's, and behind that is the bulk of the Caledonian Hotel, built around Princes Street station.**
G. M. Staddon/N. E. Stead collection

Above:
With Class 47/7 No 47712 *Lady Diana Spencer* **out of sight propelling from the rear, Mk 2f DBSO No 9705 leads the 17.30 Edinburgh-Glasgow Queen Street service through Princes Street Gardens in May 1988.**
Brian Morrison

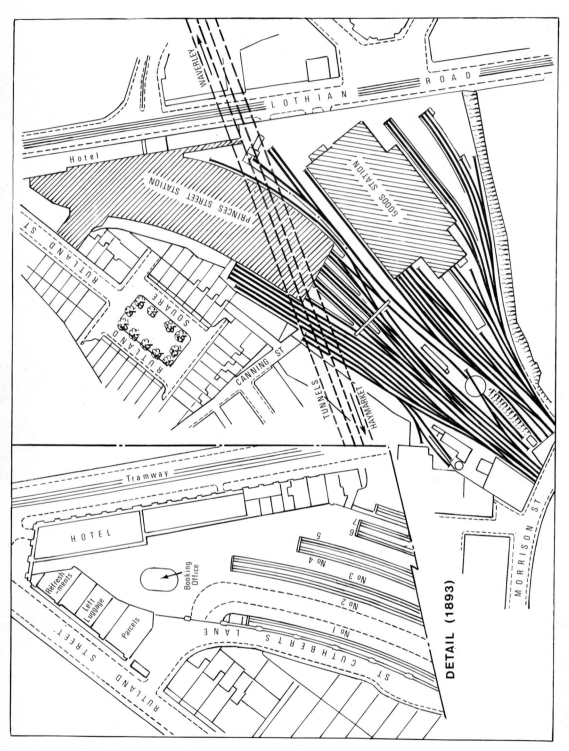

Princes Street station 1913.

WAVERLEY

LOTHIAN ROAD

Hotel

PRINCES STREET STATION

GOODS STATION

RUTLAND ST

RUTLAND SQUARE

CANNING ST

TUNNELS

HAYMARKET

MORRISON ST

DETAIL (1893)

Tramway

HOTEL

Refreshments

Left Luggage

Parcels

Booking Office

RUTLAND STREET

ST CUTHBERTS LANE

No 1

No 2

No 3

No 4

5

6

7

The first generation of Waverley-Glasgow Queen Street push-pull units were formed of two Class 27 locomotives and a rake of Mk 2 coaches. The 14.30 Glasgow-Edinburgh train approaches its destination through Princes Street Gardens in June 1977 hauled by Class 27/2 No 27201, with Class 27/1 27108 propelling out of sight at the rear. *Brian Morrison*

in rateable terms, this now-forgotten terminus was almost half the value, and therefore presumably half the ground-area, of Waverley. Princes Street station's valuation at the time of Grouping in 1923 amounted to approximately £950 — less than the rateable value of an Edinburgh suburban bungalow before the abolition of domestic rates in 1989!

A whole generation of capital citizens has grown up not knowing that once it was possible to stroll at ground-level into a station in the West End and, without plunging down any stairways or carriage-ramps as at Waverley, catch a train to London, Birmingham, Glasgow, or just to Leith. In terms of accessibility the 'Caley' was infinitely superior to Waverley, and it is tragic that no place could be found for it in the present-day railway presence in Edinburgh.

Until 1870, the Caledonian's Edinburgh terminus was at Lothian Road, almost exactly on the site now occupied by the Sheraton Hotel. This was a wooden four-platform structure, but the foundation stone laid by the Duke of Atholl had been intended for a much grander Italianate structure more appropriate for the Scottish capital. Despite its aristocratic

foundation, the new terminus was stillborn by lack of funds as a financial crisis racked the Caledonian. Indeed, in 1850, sheriff officers seized plant and equipment on behalf of frustrated creditors, and a new Act of Parliament was required to allow the company to reduce the unrealistically high dividends it had guaranteed its investors. Nor was the 'Caley's' cause in Edinburgh helped by insane competition with the Edinburgh and Glasgow for traffic between the nation's two most important cities. At one time in the 1850s second class fares between the cities were as low as 6d (2.5p) — one-eighth of a penny per mile, and absurd even by the prices of the day.

It was to be 1870 before a new terminus was built in the later situation closer to Princes Street. However, even this proved temporary — until rebuilding began in 1890 — and was described by the author W. M. Acworth as a 'wooden shanty', which might almost have been said of the building it replaced. After its destruction by fire a third attempt was made to furnish Scotland's capital with an appropriate Caledonian station.

The new building was designed by Peddie & Kinnear, and cost £120,000, according to a contemporary report. If accurate, this was less than a tenth of what the rival NBR spent on rebuilding the Waverley, although the 'Caley' terminus was, for 10 years after 1893, a long low building. Its hotel, opened in 1903, gave it its present substantial frontage at the West End (the right-hand door was the station entrance).

The Morrison Street bridge is the best vantage point for the modern citizen to glimpse what Princes

Below:
Princes Street terminus interior around 1928, looking southwestwards. Vehicles penetrated into the station from Rutland Street, out of sight to the right, while one corner of the ticket office is visible in the bottom left corner. The unusual enquiries office, crowned by cupola with clock is also visible, as is a poster advertising special fares to Aintree at 17s 6d return (87.5p in modern currency!). *Scottish Record Office*

Above:
'Britannia' Pacific No 70052 *Firth of Tay* passes through
Merchiston station on the 13.25 Saturdays-only
Glasgow Central-Princes Street train in February 1962.
This was used as a locomotive filling-in duty.
G. M. Staddon/N. E. Stead collection

Right:
Princes Street station pilot at around the turn of the
century, this unidentified Caledonian Railway 0-4-2
tender-engine was an 1870s Brittain design. Two
examples of the class survived in LMS days until the end
of the 1920s but none was allocated to Dalry Road by
the time of Grouping in 1923.   *W. E. Boyd collection*

Street passenger station, and Lothian Road goods
station, used to look like. The station's seven
platforms fanned southwestwards from a concourse
entered from Rutland Street, with pedestrians
entering from the West End pavement opposite
Princes Street corner, or up a few steps from Lothian
Road opposite King's Stables Road. Beyond the
platform ends there was a 156 lever-frame signalbox
(on the up side) and turntable between the passenger
and goods lines, the latter being on a slightly higher
level, and ending at bufferstops where the Sheraton
Hotel is situated, opposite the Usher Hall, goods
traffic having inherited the former passenger station
site.

Before going on to examine the passenger station
proper, it is worth recording the impact that this
building made on city life one Saturday night,
18 November 1939. A fire broke out in the Lothian
Road goods station that evening, highlighting the
centre of the city for any Luftwaffe bomber which
happened to be in the vicinity. Fire appliances
struggled to penetrate the huge crowds of spectators

before tackling the blaze, the fire hoses rapidly turning the station yard into a quagmire. Fourteen rail wagons were destroyed and an entire section of the south shed gutted, but fortunately there was no loss of life. However, 270 tons of chocolate were lost — no small matter in wartime.

One of the architectural features of Princes Street station was the overall steel-framed glass roof, 850ft long and 1,000ft wide at its widest point, tapering to 230ft, resting on massive red sandstone supporting walls, but with no internal pillars. This roof acted as an umbrella for the internal buildings which were nevertheless individually roofed as if for the outdoors. Most eye-catching was the building incorporating enquiries and refreshment facilities, complete with an attractive wooden cupola crowned by a clock. There was also an impressive oval booking office, with eight public windows, and a substantial kiosk, both free-standing.

Vehicular traffic could gain access to the widest, most northern, island platform from Rutland Street. The seven platforms varied in length from 460ft to 800ft, suburban services using the shorter ones on the southeastern side. There were no centre release 'roads' or loops between the platform tracks, making necessary a permanent station pilot. On the north side of the building there were five carriage sidings with low cleaning platforms between them. On this side too was an electric generator to supply lighting to the station from the time of its rebuilding.

Interestingly, the platforms were built directly above the tunnel carrying the NBR tracks between Waverley and Haymarket stations. At the time that Waverley was being expanded, and as part of their defence for keeping the Caledonian out of East Edinburgh in their quest for Leith traffic, the NBR seriously offered to build an underground exchange station at this point in their new tunnels, to allow travellers from Leith Central or existing NBR Leith stations the opportunity to gain direct access to the Caledonian system.

While such a station would undoubtedly have been an unpleasant place for staff and passengers alike, it might conceivably have offered a useful transport option in years to come, and could have lengthened the working life of Princes Street. Even at the present time, the Cockburn Association has mooted the idea of a modern station in one of the Haymarket tunnels below this point. Called 'West End', it could offer rail access to a proposed conference centre off Lothian Road, as well as increasing destination options for incoming commuter traffic from Fife, Bathgate, and the west.

It was Princes Street's buffer-stops which saw the climax to one of the most epic railway runs of all time. On the evening of 27 April 1928 a rail enthusiast on the platform awaiting the arrival of the Edinburgh portion of the 'Royal Scot' would have seen the six-coach train approaching behind Midland Compound No 1054.

For this was the consummation of a double world record for non-stop rail travel. No 1054 had run all 400 miles from London (Euston) — a record which stands to this day for a locomotive of her size — while the Glasgow portion was headed northwards over the 401-mile route to the Central station by 'Royal Scot' 4-6-0 No 6113 *Cameronian*. This was a stunt to anticipate and overshadow the LNER's introduction of non-stop running on the 'Flying Scotsman' between London and Edinburgh the following Monday. Although described by one railway historian as 'vainglorious', both runs were epics in British railroading, for the lack of corridor tenders on the LMS meant that crews could not be

Above:
Midland Compound No 1142 pauses at Slateford with a stopping train for Princes Street from Carlisle on 29 March 1926. Just over two years later sister engine No 1054 set a world record for four-coupled steam locomotives by running non-stop from Euston to Princes Street, a distance of almost exactly 400 miles.
W. E. Boyd collection

Centre right:
A brand-new NB Loco-built 'Royal Scot' 4-6-0, No 6128 (later *Meteor*, and after 1936, *The Lovat Scouts*) without nameplate and with burnished buffers, pauses at Kingsknowe while running in on a Glasgow (Central)-Edinburgh (Princes Street) slow in the summer of 1927. 'Royal Scots' were not common visitors to Edinburgh. Note the Caledonian train-identity semaphore code shown above the buffer-beam. *C. Highet collection, SRO*

Bottom right:
Former Caledonian Class 60 4-6-0 No 54638 takes the Holytown and Glasgow direction at Midcalder Junction, leaving the link to the WCML through Carstairs in the foreground. The time is August 1949, not long before a number of these engines were reallocated to the 'Lion's Den' of the rival North British former headquarters, St Margarets. *Real Photos*

Left:
The red LMS livery, and the removal of the smokebox wingplates, cannot disguise the lines of 4-6-0 No 14750, seen at Slateford on the 10.35 Glasgow (Central) slow to Princes Street on 16 April 1925. This engine was none other than the former Caledonian No 49, whose introduction in 1903 caused a sensation among railway observers, because of its size. Note the eight-wheeled tender, necessary for running on the WCML which had no water-troughs between Carlisle and Glasgow until LMS days. *W. E. Boyd collection*

Above:
Diverted via Carlisle because of the Penmanshiel Tunnel collapse, Class 55 No 55009 *Alycidon* approaches the city from the west over the former Caledonian Slateford viaduct with the 23.15 King's Cross-Waverley sleeper on 9 August 1979. The reason for the unidentified Class 20 pilot is not known. *M. Macdonald*

changed without stopping. Obviously, such a feat of endurance could not be asked of engine crews in normal conditions and the LNER's 'Flying Scotsman' service in and out of Waverley was the longest scheduled non-stop run in the world. But *Cameronian's* record, although beaten by an American diesel a few years later, stood for international steam traction for 20 years — and it was to be Edinburgh crews who beat it, no fewer than 17 times. But more of that later.

The Caledonian Railway, and its successor in Edinburgh, the LMS, was not ungenerous in its provision of suburban trains in and out of Princes Street. As late as 1938 the Merchiston district, which in our own time has had to get along without trains now for more than 25 years, had between 38 and 40 train arrivals or departures in the average day. Murrayfield was even better served, with no fewer than 65 trains calling daily in each direction. This compares almost exactly with those LNER services stopping at Portobello on the other side of the city, although that station also had 15 trains daily to that other major Edinburgh station, Leith Central.

Right to the end of its life the 'Caley' was signalled with semaphores, despite being re-equipped by the LMS as late as 1937, utilising the existing box, at the same time that its rival company was resignalling the Waverley area with colour lights. Steam locomotives blackened its roof until the last day, with DMUs on the Leith branch services being the only regular diesel representatives. The atmosphere was totally different from Waverley, with no through traffic, and long spells of apparent inactivity.

One peculiarity for young postwar train-spotters, accustomed to the gleaming Pacifics and later Deltics which populated the Waverley, was the sight of London and Birmingham expresses often arriving at or leaving Princes Street behind 2-6-4T engines. These powered the trains as far as Carstairs or

Symington where the coaches would be attached to the corresponding southbound service from Glasgow or even Aberdeen, but the tanks were no slouches, often attaining speeds larger engines would be proud of. In contrast, former LMS Pacifics from Polmadie could often be seen 'filling in' on comparatively light trains to and from Glasgow (Central). For example in the spring of 1938 rail enthusiasts frequenting the 'Caley' station in the evenings would see then-new streamlined 'Coronation' Pacifics regularly working in on the 18.45 ex-Glasgow Central, returning on the 21.30.

A unique biennial feature of this almost forgotten station was the arrival of numerous special trains from Wales for the traditional international rugby fixture at Murrayfield. Modern locomotives from Crewe depot are frequently seen in the city nowadays but this was certainly not normally the case during the life of the 'Caley' station, and the arrival of exotic 'Jubilees', 'Royal Scots' and 'Patriots' was eagerly awaited by enthusiasts. In 1935 the match generated no fewer than 35 specials from Wales in the preceding few days, 20 of them originating from GWR stations and the rest from the LMS. Many rugby specials from other parts of Scotland frequently went through directly to Murrayfield station on the Leith North branch on the day of the match, utilising the Slateford-Murrayfield spur which crossed the former NBR lines at Russell Road east of Haymarket depot.

Rationalisation of Scottish railways inevitably led to the demise of Princes Street station, with many of

Above:
Waverley was not the only Edinburgh station that boasted Pacifics. Stanier No 46221 *Queen Elizabeth* steams out of Princes Street station with a local train to Glasgow Central in 1960. *N. E. Stead collection*

Below:
Caledonian 4-4-0 No 54504 approaches Princes Street station in July 1955 with the 13.25 from Stirling.
G. M. Staddon/N. E. Stead collection

its services gradually being transferred to Waverley. Only Leith North — the last passenger station to serve the port — could not be directly duplicated by services from Waverley. When closed in 1962, it was the last suburban terminus reached from Princes Street, others such as Barnton and Balerno already having vanished from the railway map (in 1951 and 1943 respectively).

The building of the Duff Street connection now hastened the end of the 'Caley', providing a route for Waverley departures from the southwestern platform end of Haymarket to the former Caledonian Slateford-Murrayfield spur by way of that company's former Haymarket (goods) branch, and thence to the rest of that system. With the withdrawal of the Leith service, it was only a matter of finding accommodation for the remaining 'Caley' services at Waverley. All Sunday services were transferred there in 1962, using the suburban circle and the new Craiglockhart-Slateford link until the Duff Street connection was available in 1965.

So Edinburgh lost a magnificent, underused, transport option. Waverley cannot match the 'Caley' for its sheer ease of accessibility — something which was not enough to save from closure this once-busy terminus with its 200 staff and five trains daily to London (Euston).

Haymarket-western approaches

Nowadays fulfilling a dual role as a railhead for much of western Edinburgh, and as a transfer station for traffic between Glasgow and Fife, Haymarket remains just as busy as it once must have been when it was the eastern terminus of the Edinburgh and Glasgow Railway. Certainly, in 1984/85 it was Scotland's twelfth top station for revenue, although that statistic cannot quantify the station's considerable convenience as a transfer point.

Always distinguished architecturally, Haymarket station no longer boasts the iron train shed immediately to the north of the modern running lines. This was the original E&G terminus, dating from 1842, and was saved for posterity by the Scottish Railway Preservation Society which has now integrated the venerable structure — described by the Ancient Monuments Archive as 'formed with fluted cast-iron columns and elliptical arches with decorated spandrels' — into its Bo'ness branch terminus.

The station's façade facing the main Glasgow road is greatly improved by stone-cleaning and can now be imagined in its original role as the headquarters of a small, although busy, railway. In 1842 one traveller deemed it 'a splendid and imposing structure, with a handsome colonnade in front'. The Penguin *Buildings of Scotland* guide describes the building as 'domestic in form but heavy in detail except for the tetrastyle Tuscan porch'. The E&G boardroom apparently still exists upstairs, complete with 'monumental granite chimneypiece'.

However, the 'business' end of the station has always been functional to the point of depressing austerity, although not so bad now as in the days of steam. Towards the end of the last century, W. M. Acworth followed his pungent comments about Waverley by observing that Haymarket 'which was opened in 1842, had remained untouched, except the platforms — it may have been painted, but it shows no signs of it'. Unfortunately, this impression was still prevalent for nearly another 100 years or so. The wooden platform canopies have now vanished, not a change to be greatly regretted. The main station building itself now claims to be the second oldest in continual BR use.

Before the eastward extension of the E&G by tunnel to Princes Street Gardens and Waverley, and some 50 years before Acworth delivered his opinion of Haymarket, local author W. H. Lizars gave us a fascinating account of an Edinburgh-Glasgow journey which contrasts somewhat with the present-day shuttle-like service between the cities.

> 'The train being now in motion, we proceed along the line, passing on the right the extensive carriage and goods sheds belonging to the Company, and on the left, the first signal, which consists of pointed vanes by day, and a lamp with coloured glass by night. About a quarter of a mile from the starting point, on the right, we pass the Water Tank, for supplying the locomotive engines, which is itself supplied from a well dug close by . . .'

Haymarket depot, thus described, is not in fact on the site of the present-day 'Sprinter' depot which is situated in the Murrayfield/Roseburn districts of the city, some way by road from Haymarket station itself. The original depot was sited opposite the turn-off of the Caledonian branch from Slateford to the brewing establishments of the area, although Ordnance survey maps show a direct Caledonian connection into Haymarket's southern (terminal) platform until the 1890s, thus comfortably predating the Duff Street connection. Of this more anon, while Haymarket depot will receive its rightful consideration later.

Although its main-line between the cities was, and still is, 47 miles long, by the end of the 1850s the enterprising Edinburgh & Glasgow Railway Company owned three times that route-mileage, as well as 32 miles of the Union Canal and a lease of the Edinburgh & Bathgate Railway. It held a crucial place in the development of Scottish railways, owning as it did the shortest and potentially

Above:
North British 'Scott' class 4-4-0 No 62418 *The Pirate*
hauls the 7.25pm Waverley-Anstruther local out of
Haymarket in July 1956. This was a regular working for
North British 4-4-0s at the time.
G. M. Staddon/N. E. Stead collection

quickest route across the central belt. Because of its strategic position straddling this Scottish isthmus it attracted a large number of Lancastrian shareholders who had already seen demonstrated the value of a short inter-city line — between Liverpool and Manchester.

Unfortunately, the E&G's early years seem to have been marred by boardroom squabbling and downright mismanagement, otherwise this company would surely have been ideally based for further rail developments of its own in Central Scotland. As it was, it represented the launching-pad for either the Caledonian or the North British to attack the other's stronghold in either Glasgow or Edinburgh respectively, although, in truth, until the NBR somewhat surprisingly outwitted its rival and merged with the E&G in 1865, the NB really held little more than a peripheral grip on the Scottish railway scene up to that year. Indeed, had the Caledonian taken over the Edinburgh & Glasgow, its eastern rival, the NBR, would surely have been nothing more than a southern equivalent of the Great North of Scotland Railway. The 'Caley' would then have owned two main lines between Glasgow and Edinburgh, one of them reaching into Waverley, where, in the event, its only presence was to be by running powers until the 1890s.

Initially, E&G services between the two Scottish cities comprised six trains each way, taking 2¼hr on the journey, plus an early morning 'luggage train' in each direction taking 3½hr. Additionally, and most controversially, there were two trains every Sunday. The company soon came to a working arrangement with the Union Canal before absorbing it in 1849, amid more boardroom recriminations. This helped remove passenger competition from the railway,

although freight continued to use the waterway until 1933. Interestingly, had the E&G felt so minded in the 1850s, it might have seen the Union Canal's eastern terminus, at Port Hopetoun, a couple of hundred yards up Lothian Road from the Caledonian's original terminus, as a potential rail terminal, with useful siding space available for local industries and particularly the meat-markets. As it was, the North British Railway finally curtailed the canal in 1922 at its present western basin immediately to the southwest of West Fountainbridge. The site of Port Hopetoun was filled in around 1923, and this remained vacant for a surprisingly long period until the construction of Lothian House in 1935-36.

Change at Haymarket

When on a recent visit to Haymarket station, the author was startled to hear a juvenile Liverpudlian voice ask the booking-clerk for a half-single to Edinburgh! Three more youngsters made a similar request in the same accent, the clerk seeming to be unsurprised by the request for tickets to Edinburgh — from travellers who were standing within 5min walk of Princes Street! The phenomenon can probably be explained by the fact that passengers arriving on trains from Lancashire, the Midlands and the Southwest are often ill-informed enough to

Top left:
'A3' Pacific No 60095 *Flamingo* exits from Edinburgh to the Fife lines at Haymarket Central in July 1960. This was a Carlisle engine, which was unusual working west of Edinburgh. *G. M. Staddon/N. E. Stead collection*

Centre left:
'V1' and 'V3' 2-6-2Ts were standard motive power on the Scottish capital's suburban trains in and out of Waverley before dieselisation began in 1958. Here 'V1' No 67630 heads a stopping train past the Inner Circle turn-off at Haymarket Central Junction in the early 1950s. *J. Robertson*

Bottom left:
Almost brand-new, NBR 'Scott' 4-4-0 No 498 *Father Ambrose* heads a Glasgow express past Haymarket Central Junction in 1920. This locomotive survived until August 1958. *Real Photos*

Above:
Only three years old, NBR Class 'J' 4-4-0 (later LNER 'D30') No 501 *Simon Glover* is seen running light at Saughton Junction about 1923. The engine is on the Glasgow (Queen Street)/Larbert down line, with the Aberdeen line about to fork off northwards. *Real Photos*

alight at Haymarket when they really want Waverley. Perhaps ScotRail's guards could be more informative in their train announcements, stressing Haymarket's virtues as a transfer station for trains to the north and west — especially valuable if the arrival from the Carstairs direction is running late — but telling those passengers wishing to visit the city itself to stay on until Waverley is reached.

Mention has already been made of Haymarket's value as a transfer point, and an example of this should now be given. At the time of writing, arrivals from Glasgow (Queen Street) normally reach Haymarket at 14min and 44min past the hour. This means that a Glaswegian travelling to the Fife Coast

on the on-the-hour departure from Queen Street has only a few minutes to wait for a Kirkcaldy/Dundee train at 49min past the hour, thus giving a fast hourly service between Glasgow and Kirkcaldy in 88min, of which only five are spent awaiting a connection. It should be emphasised that not since 1972 have through services operated regularly between Queen Street and Fife, travelling via the Winchburgh-Dalmeny loop and the Forth Bridge.

In the opposite direction, a Kirkcaldy resident travelling to Glasgow will have approximately 16min to wait at Haymarket, giving a journey time some 15min short of 2hr. The above example actually allows the traveller time to catch his or her train at Waverley, although late running has to be allowed for, and it must be said, Haymarket, now replete with refreshment facilities, is a more pleasant place at which to change trains than at any time in living memory. In addition, it has a new claim to fame as the first station to be modernised in a custom-built open arrangement.

Haymarket is very much a working station, but has lost one of its main attractions for the enthusiast — the movement of light engines between Haymarket depot and Waverley. This traffic has lessened with the introduction of IC125s operating out of Craigentinny, whose use on expresses from starting-points north and west of Edinburgh to King's Cross has given Haymarket an impressive array of departures to the London terminus. It is not unknown for regular East Coast passengers to board busy southbound expresses at Haymarket instead of Waverley during such peak travelling times as the weekends of the Festival. Standing in the train while it traverses the centre of Edinburgh guarantees these wily travellers a prior place in the scramble for unreserved seats when passengers from the north alight at a Waverley platform solid with waiting passengers bound for London.

4
Rails to the North

By tunnel to Aberdeen

One day in 1983 a mechanical digger, clearing the Waverley Market site to accommodate a new shopping mall, unearthed the mouth of a tunnel disappearing northwards under Princes Street. This was probably the last appearance of the south end of the railway tunnel which ran from Canal Street to Scotland Street, and which still exists under the city, almost totally forgotten save for a small sign on the north wall of Waverley.

But this was no suburban underground line; no Victorian local rapid-transit link within the city. It was designed and built as a trunk route connecting Edinburgh with Dundee and Aberdeen, and had a working life of around 21 years. Canal Street, now buried under the Waverley Centre shopping mall, was the terminus of the Edinburgh Leith & Newhaven Railway (later the Edinburgh Leith & Granton, and later still the Edinburgh Perth & Dundee and North British Railways), and until 1868 was a railhead for those points north of the Forth, connecting with the Granton-Burntisland ferry link. And what a way to start a journey to the north!

The tunnel (1,000yd long, 24ft wide and 17ft high) to Scotland Street plunged under the New Town on a downward gradient of 1 in 27, so a northbound journey must have been like a journey into Hades. Grinding down the incline, the passenger coaches were steadied by brake trucks, while in the up direction there was an endless rope, running under rollers between the rails. All these did the work of locomotives, none of which entered the portal of the gaslit tunnel at Scotland Street. Power was supplied by a stationary steam engine at the prematurely-named Canal Street. (This site may have been intended for an ornamental canal as part of James Craig's plans for the New Town, and the later Union Canal never reached this part of the city, terminating instead at Port Hopetoun, now the site of the Cannon cinema in Lothian Road.) There was a station at Scotland Street, before a second tunnel was entered under Rodney Street.

In 1862 the company was taken over by the North British Railway which was anxious to be rid of this problem feature of its network and constructed the Abbeyhill line in 1868, to take trains from Waverley to Granton or Leith. Rail access to Scotland Street

continued from the northern direction until the late 1960s to service a coal depot there.

But even if no longer part of the NBR's system, the tunnel still played a vital role in that company's development. The Caledonian's 1890 proposal for an underground line beneath the length of Princes Street and then on down to Leith threatened the North British's monopoly of east Edinburgh, indeed of southeast Scotland. This proposal came at a bad time for the NBR, which was financially stretched by its participation in the construction of the Forth Bridge and in preparing its rebuilding plans for Waverley.

Here, Scotland Street tunnel came to the rescue. By showing that the Caledonian's projected underground line physically intruded on the tunnel, the Edinburgh company was able to see off the 'Caley' threat, much to the delight of citizens horrified at the proposals for railway tracks running under the length of Princes Street. (Indeed, the plans for the Princes Street underground line were not a paradigm of draughtsmanship, also showing an unrealistically sharp curve at the western end.) Although the NB implied to a Parliamentary committee that the Scotland Street tunnel was a potentially vital part of its network, its only function at this time was for growing mushrooms!

A visitor who inspected the tunnel in March 1889 found two lines of rails still in place, the down line being covered over by horticultural sectioned culture-beds which were removed bodily and renewed every six months. The air entering from Scotland Street was warmed by an anthracite fire burning in the tunnel mouth, and it must have seemed that the Edinburgh Mushroom Co had found an ideal environment for its product. This was the company name for the enterprise for at least one stage of its history, although there appear to have been a succession of concerns involved. Business archives show that the Scottish Mushroom Co was also active under the city's streets at one time, one of its shareholders in 1899 being the Scotland Street station agent, who was well-placed to keep an eye on his investment! In later years, unfortunately, the crop was irreversibly affected by a parasite.

While a single line of rails – complete with rollers for the tow-rope – existed under the capital's streets at least until 1938, the structure's main usefulness

Above:
Easter Road station, on the line from London Road Junction to Granton, was visited by a rail tour in August 1963. The motive power was St Margaret's 'J37' 0-6-0 No 64624. *G. M. Staddon/N. E. Stead collection*

was in providing a bombproof centre for LNER Control headquarters during World War 2. Running water and electricity were laid on, and subsidiary tunnels dug for additional accommodation for up to 3,000 staff who were protected during air-raids by specially-installed blastproof doors.

After the war, the tunnel was chosen by an Edinburgh University physicist as an ideal location to test equipment for isolating and measuring non-terrestrial atomic particles. The scientist involved may have been embarrassed by the local newspaper headlines announcing this experiment as 'Edinburgh's forgotten tunnel enters Nuclear Age' sensation – for the Scottish Nobel Prizewinner C. T. R. Wilson had used the Caledonian rail tunnel at Neidpath near Peebles for a remarkably similar purpose before World War 1!

Scotland Street's tunnel was later used for car storage, and was ingeniously employed as a getaway route for mail-bag thieves in 1979, following a robbery at Waverley. The crime involved the removal of a number of mailbags from one of the Waverley's northern platforms, the 'loot' being secreted down the tunnel where it was quickly recovered near the far portal. No financial loss was reported, and access to the tunnel bore made more secure.

In contrast to the southern end of the tunnel, the northern portal still towers over a children's adventure playground at Scotland Street. The attractive southern outline of the Rodney Street tunnel portal stands opposite its longer counterpart a few yards away, but this short tunnel is also blocked, at its northern end by a new housing development at Heriothill, where the EL&G Co had its first workshops. Walkways now extend along the former tracks from this latter point, northwards towards Trinity, and Leith-wards through Warriston cemetery, where an ornamental overbridge carries joggers and dog-walkers above the graves.

The lines running northwards from Heriothill in two directions were rendered obsolete as trunk routes by the building in 1868 of the line from London Road Junction, near Abbeyhill, to both Granton and North Leith stations. The newer line (providing, at one time, stations at Easter Road, Leith Walk, and for a comparatively short time, at Powderhall) existed in a greatly overgrown condition until very recently (winter 1985/86) to carry occasional naphtha traffic to Granton Gasworks. It was crossed on the level, by the North Leith line which it replaced, by way of one of Scotland's rare rail-crossings: the branch now ends a couple of hundred yards up the trackbed from this point.

Effectively, the whole of the original (Scotland Street) line into Edinburgh was redundant as anything but a goods link, Heriothill retaining a goods depot manager in the city's postal directories until 1923, while the Scotland Street coal depot lasted until November 1967.

Granton: One-time Gateway to the north

From around 1846 until the opening of the Forth Bridge in 1890, Granton was the easiest and quickest means for the Edinburgh rail traveller to reach the 'wee kingdom' of Fife, as well as more distant localities such as Dundee and Aberdeen. The Granton-Burntisland ferry provided this link, using unprecedented technology, and was still offering a service into the 1950s, although not for rail traffic.

After the Scotland Street tunnel closed to regular traffic in 1868, Granton traffic began and finished its journeys at the eastern platforms of the Waverley station, proceeding through the Calton tunnel and then through Abbeyhill and under Leith Walk, across the North Leith branch by the level-crossing already mentioned to join the existing line at Trinity Junction.

From 1849 the ferry arrangements at Granton were unique in pioneering 'roll-on, roll-off', facilities for rail vehicles, comprising the world's first public train-ferry service (although a coal-carrying example existed at Blyth in Northumberland from 1842-51). A wheel-mounted ramp could be moved up and down the Granton slipway, depending on the height of the tide, to allow rail vehicles to gain level access with the tracks specially fitted to the deck of the ferry *Leviathan*. There was no mollycoddling of all the embarking passengers however – unless they were travelling first class they simply made themselves as comfortable as they could on deck amongst the vehicles! For this privilege, the fare was 6d (2.5p) for steerage, or twice as much for a cabin.

As the 1840s drew to a close, the ferry service comprised boats leaving Granton on weekdays at 06.50, 10.05, 12.50, 16.35 and 18.35, with both passengers and freight being conveyed. There were departures from Burntisland at 08.10, 12.45, 15.10, and 17.40. Surprisingly, the service operated on Sundays too – at 07.50, 13.00 and 16.50, underlining its importance as a trunk route.

The integral place held by the Granton ferry service in the Scottish transport scene before 1890 was illustrated by the need for no fewer than nine vessels to operate it at one time – four passenger and five freight. The operators (for most of the ferry's life, the NBR) were also catering for non-rail traffic, charging from 1d for ferrying a dog, up to 15s (75p)

Below:
An unusual photograph of the wooden Granton station, probably in the 1920s. *J. H. Sutherland*

for a hearse complete with driver and two horses. This ferry connection was probably the quickest means of crossing the Forth until the opening of the Forth Bridge in 1890.

After that year, one NBR-operated vessel sufficed for the reduced ferry service between Granton and Burntisland, all rail traffic using the new bridge. This one vessel, the Kinghorn-built *William Muir,* became a local institution, plying the Forth waters for nearly 60 years to total 800,000 miles on withdrawal in March 1937. The ferry link came to an end in 1940 when Granton became a minesweeping base, two postwar efforts to revive the service in 1950 and 1955, using converted landing-craft, proving commercially unsuccessful. This is somewhat surprising, given the increasing pressure on the anachronistically-limited Queensferry service under the shadow of the rail bridge before the Forth Road Bridge opened in 1964.

The passenger service to and from Granton – and the saga of its bungled closure by the LNER – will be dealt with later.

The Forth Rail Bridge

'The finest bridge in all of England' – this was the instinctive reaction of a southern visitor to his first sight of the Forth Rail Bridge at Queensferry. His geographical inaccuracy is perhaps almost matched by this author's for including the bridge in a survey of Edinburgh's railways. For this great construction is the best part of 10 miles from Waverley station and originally connected Linlithgowshire (West Lothian) with Fife. Following local government reorganisation in 1974 however, Edinburgh District now encompasses South Queensferry, so no further excuse is surely necessary to include the Forth Bridge in this book.

For this is *the* Forth Bridge, now in to its second century. Handsome though its partner road bridge is, three-quarters of a mile upriver, the rail bridge takes some beating as a symbol of majestic but functional solidity. C. Hamilton Ellis waxed lyrical about the bridge in his book *The North British Railway* (Ian Allan Ltd), making the point that 'its beauty is unconscious, as in so many Victorian structures'. Small wonder it has been the locus of derring-do in such films as *The Thirty-Nine Steps* (a NBR Atlantic can just be spotted in the earlier Hitchcock version), and a priority target for the Luftwaffe in the early part of World War 2.

Any account of the Bridge can easily become a wearying recitation of construction statistics, so only the salient points will be listed here. Sited at the Queensferry Narrows, which a glance at a map will soon show is the lowest short crossing-point of this great estuary, the Bridge was not the first structure proposed to carry rail traffic into Fife from the south.

Sir Thomas Bouch, the ill-starred builder of the first Tay Bridge was already drawing up his plans for the Forth crossing, when disaster struck in 1879, and 70 souls were lost in the stormy Firth of Tay. Many of them had travelled from Edinburgh on the Granton-Burntisland ferry link which Bouch was working to eradicate. Not surprisingly, the Tay Bridge disaster effectively killed off Bouch's proposals for Queensferry, ending his career and possibly contributing to his early death.

But Victorian railway administrators were not the kind of men likely to be intimidated by the most horrendous railway disaster in British history. A consortium comprising the NBR, NER, GNR, and Midland railways commissioned a cantilever bridge design by Benjamin Baker and Sir John Fowler. The leading contractor was William Arrol, and construction began in 1883.

After seven years work, and at a cost of 57 workmen's lives, the Prince of Wales hammered in a golden rivet to signal the opening of the great structure to rail traffic on 4 March 1890. One and a half miles long, towering 341ft above sea level, the Bridge consumed nearly two-thirds of a million cu ft of Aberdeen granite, 54,000 tons of steel, and 62,000cu ft of rubble masonry. The statistics go on and on: the Bridge itself seems immortal. In its first year more than 20,000 passenger, and nearly 30,000 freight trains rumbled over the Forth and the cumulative total since then would doubtless be yet another enormous statistic.

Administered by the Forth Bridge Co until nationalisation with the railways from 1 January 1948, the costs were shared 30% by the North British, 32.5% by the Midland, with the Great Northern and North Eastern each contributing 18.75%. Its completion made possible the 1895 Railway Race to Aberdeen, and gave the East Coast partner companies the shortest route to the northern cities beyond the Tay. How ironic that the Midland should have paid almost twice as much as either of its English partners in the FBC! The modern reader is forced to speculate if such investment could possibly have been worth Derby's while, for within 15 years the Midland was having to pay the NBR subsidies to maintain a full timetable of Anglo-Scottish services over the Waverley Route.

It was, and still is, a glorious monument to 19th century engineering. Just past its centenary, it simply has to be seen to be believed. It is debatable which makes the greater impression – travelling across the Forth at a height great enough to allow the world's tallest warships to sail beneath, or simply viewing the Bridge from ground level, with the rumble of trains echoing across the water.

If you have never seen the Forth Bridge, you have still to appreciate the Railway Age which has passed us by.

Above:
Fish traffic from the northern Scottish ports to London now appears to favour road transport but was once given almost express passenger treatment by the railways. In this 1950s picture a Dundee 'V2' 2-6-2, No 60958 heads an up train across the Forth Bridge.
Real Photos

Left:
Having crossed the Forth Bridge, Class 150/2 Sprinter No 150262 enters Dalmeny station forming the 11.45 Waverley to Waverley service via Dunfermline and Cowdenbeath in December 1989. *Brian Morrison*

Above right:
Crossing the North Approach Viaduct of the Forth Bridge and about to enter the Fife Cantilever, a seemingly diminutive Class 47/4 No 47460 *University of Strathclyde* heads the 08.45 Aberdeen-Plymouth train, the 'Devon Scot', in May 1988. *Brian Morrison*

Right:
Thompson Class B1 4-6-0 No 61357 hauls a mixed goods out of Dalmeny in June 1958, with the Forth Bridge in the background. *G. M. Staddon/N. E. Stead collection*

5

Racing Days

Mention has already been made of Edinburgh's part in the Railway Races to the North in 1888 and 1895. Both incidents have been graphically recounted by O. S. Nock in his Ian Allan book *The Railway Race to the North* published in 1959, and the interested reader is recommended to read it.

Suffice to say that inter-company rivalry between the East and West Coast routes led to two exciting tussles to be first from London to Edinburgh in 1888, and to Aberdeen in 1895. Railway enthusiasts were agog with excitement as timetables were torn to shreds, running times reduced to unbelievable levels, and some highly dangerous passing speeds recorded! The logistical problem of which terminus to visit, at opposite ends of Princes Street, in order to welcome in the first of the racers, was one which must have seated Edinburgh rail buffs on the horns of a painful dilemma!

In 1888 Edinburgh came within 7hr 27min of London, a time which included a passenger lunch-break, and stops for locomotive water supply. Seven years later, with Edinburgh reduced to the role of an East Coast engine-change point in the overnight race to Aberdeen, a time of 8hr 40min from London to the Granite City was recorded, the West Coast having cut even this by some 8min. On this second competitive occasion, no meal stops were made. One footnote in Edinburgh's involvement in the 1895 race was the 81½mph recorded by the North Eastern 4-4-0 No 1621 over a 15mph speed restriction at Portobello!

Six years later, another race developed to Edinburgh; one on which historians are not completely in agreement. Both O. S. Nock and Cecil J. Allen believed that there was no race at all in 1901, mainly because one of the 'racers' appeared so obviously outclassed. This was the published opinion of none other than the great Charles Rous-Martin, the eminent railway journalist who had nearly been converted to jam (in his words) in Portobello's Duddingston Road during the 1895 incident. So reputable was Rous-Martin that his opinion on anything was usually the 'received' one, and so the 1901 episode has not until recently been given the attention it deserves.

For in that year, a competition blew up between the North Eastern and the North British Railways to bring their afternoon express arrivals into Waverley

before each other. The North Eastern was operating the 'Flying Scotsman' into the heart of Scotland's capital thanks to running powers it held over NBR metals north of Berwick-on-Tweed, while the latter company was bringing in the 09.30 ex-St Pancras into Waverley over the route of the same name after taking the express over from the Midland at Carlisle.

The trouble was that the St Pancras arrival was scheduled to be some 10min ahead (at 18.05) of the King's Cross train at Waverley and the NER feared delays at Portobello East Junction, where the East Coast and Waverley routes joined. In reply, the North Eastern decided to clip 15min off their express's travelling time (in so doing breaching the 1896 understanding between East and West Coast Routes), thus unofficially scheduling an Edinburgh arrival time of 18.00.

The scene was set, the first week in July 1901, for a race to be first into the Scottish capital.

As events rapidly proved, the North Eastern was not a company to tangle with. Day after day the railway enthusiasts crowding the platform ends at Waverley saw NER green emerge from the Calton tunnels before NBR gamboge. Not once in that first week of racing did the local company put up a serious challenge to the work of the NER 'R' class 4-4-0 No 2015 and her sisters.

By the Friday of that week Rous-Martin told his readers of *The Engineer* magazine that there was no race to speak of. This was to dismiss some magnificent running by the North British, even it was having to settle for second place against a rival with a more favourable main line and a tradition of high-speed running. Twelve years before the 1901 episode made headlines, the much-travelled railway author W. M. Acworth had commended the standard of Waverley Route running by the NBR. In his book *The Railways of Scotland*, he asks:

'What the *Chemin de fer du Nord* authorities, who cannot manage to keep time with their expresses from Paris to Amiens at some 40mph, would think of hauling over this road (the Waverley Route) the heavy Pullmans of the Midland down Highland expresses, in 140 minutes without a stop one really would like to know. Probably they would think what a nuisance competition was . . .'

'Competition' was certainly the right word for what motivated the protagonists of 1901 (when the timing on the Waverley Route was down to 135min), and how delightful to see this Scottish railway being so favourably viewed in a European context!

We know of at least one occasion when an 'M' class 4-4-0 No 738 ran the Waverley Route non-stop in 126min with about 150 tons behind the tender, which, incidentally, held only 3,500gal of water, not an over-generous amount when Whitrope and Falahill had to be climbed. Indeed, on one day of that week the Midland was forced to stop at Blea Moor for water on its Settle-Carlisle section, yet the Scottish company still regained time north of Carlisle. So historians who write off the 1901 race as being one-sided are being unfair to the old North British.

They are also being inaccurate. On Friday 5 July, the race became *three*-sided.

Unlike the two previous outbursts of racing, 1901 involved three competitors, totalling five companies. The Midland and North British, quite uninten-

tionally it appears, had triggered the conflict with the North Eastern, whose ally the Great Northern, remained aloof from the competition. But on that Friday, as the North Eastern brought the 'Flying Scotsman' into Edinburgh 3min ahead of its rival, it discovered that it was having to settle for second-best.

A mile to the west, in Princes Street station, a Caledonian 'Dunalastair III' had just brought off a spectacular run over Beattock and Cobbinshaw summits in 97 or 98min net for the 100.5 miles from Carlisle. No less than 35min early, No 899 of the city's Dalry Road depot was greeted by platforms empty of porters and railway enthusiasts. The latter were all understandably at Waverley, while the surprise among the Caledonian Railway's own staff at Princes Street was only exceeded by those of the signalling staff in the Beattock area, where, incredibly, the train had been stopped twice by signals for a reported total of 8min. Needless to say, No 899 and her crew had brought to a conclusion the fastest recorded daytime London-Edinburgh run of the year, and possible one of the fastest ever made by a steam engine between the Border city and the Scottish capital.

The North Eastern responded immediately, bringing the overnight 20.15 ex-King's Cross into Edinburgh in 7hr 36min — 4min faster than the LNWR/CR initiative of the previous day. Whether this would have elicited an even greater response from the West Coast is a moot point. The weekend's intervention, with so much excursion traffic in Scotland and the North of England, gave the companies time to draw breath, and prevented a second whole week of rivalry, although it was the West Coast which won again on the Saturday.

Pictured early in 1925, Gresley 'A1' Pacific No 2564 accelerates an up train through Portobello East Junction. The locomotive is still unnamed (it was soon to be *Knight of the Thistle,* **with the** *'the'* **later incorrectly omitted), and has right-hand drive configuration, something which Edinburgh author Norman McKillop argued had evolved historically from drivers in the early years of railroading being in the habit of passing to one another information about possible obstacles on the line ahead.** *Real Photos*

Monday 8 July saw an interesting development, with the North British winning at last — although possibly more by foul means than fair! The setting for this last round of railway racing across the Border was Portobello East Junction in Edinburgh's eastern suburbs, greatly reduced in importance nowadays compared to 1901.

During its heyday the East Junction was the principal joining of routes on the east side of the capital. Not only was it the junction of two major lines to London, but it also gave trains from Portobello access to the Suburban Circle, and its box (an overhead gantry cabin from 1909) controlled a double-track turnout from Portobello yards and through tracks from the South Leith branch.

But to return to that July evening when the 'Flying Scotsman' and the 09.30 ex-St Pancras were belled as approaching the junction at exactly the same moment! On that occasion the signalman in the 45-lever box on the south side of the tracks at Portobello East may have been in something of a quandary.

Was history to repeat itself? Would the signalman at Portobello follow the alleged example of his counterpart at Kinnaber Junction in 1895, when the racing trains approached his box simultaneously on the last stage of the race to Aberdeen? Legend has it that the Kinnaber signalman, a Caledonian employee, sportingly gave the road to the rival North British train when both approached his box at the same time.

There was never the remotest chance of such a thing happening at Portobello. The Midland/North British was, after all, timetabled to arrive before the North Eastern's train, whose 18.00 expected arrival time at Waverley was unofficial. There were numerous records of NER-powered trains north of Berwick being delayed by NBR-operated signals whenever published schedules were being improved upon.

In November 1900, a Class S 4-6-0 on the northbound 'Flying Scotsman' was deliberately delayed at Berwick for some 18min (while the passengers 'fumed and made indignant remarks' reported *The Times*). When the signal was finally pulled 'off' on that occasion the 4-6-0's spirited crew made up 14min before being obstructed again on the outskirts of Edinburgh. Similarly, on the first day of the 1901 racing episode, the King's Cross train was held up for some 7min in the vicinity of Berwick, and one can only speculate that the NBR signal staff were giving their company's No 738, on the St Pancras, all the help they could!

While the North British company's attitude may have appeared unsporting, it should be remembered that their York-based rival was not keeping to the 8hr 15min schedule limit it had agreed to in 1896 for Anglo-Scottish services. So there was really no doubt which of the two trains approaching Portobello East on 8 July would sight a signal at danger, and the first livery to emerge from the Calton tunnel into Waverley a few minutes later, dead on time, was the mustard-like gamboge of the NBR.

The *Scotsman* newspaper had a reporter on the platform every evening at this time, and he reported that the NER train arrived only 4min later, having been held at Portobello for 4min. This is interesting, for it suggests that if anything, the NER train was first to reach the junction. Portobello East is 3½ miles from Waverley, although the tracks then wound round the south side of Portobello station, regaining something like their present alignment at the Baileyfield Road overbridge with a fairly tight curve. For this distance 4-4½min was really good progress to Waverley pass to stop, with about 6min being realistic for a start-to-stop performance for a train held at the junction. Thus, if the NBR train was punctual it must have passed the East junction at between 18.00 and 18.01, while the North Eastern train would have restarted from stop at around 18.03. This, after a 4min signal delay means an arrival at Portobello East, after braking for some distance, at about 17.59. No prizes for guessing who really won the race that evening!

In fact, describing the 'Flying Scotsman' as the 'North Eastern' train is inaccurate, since it was composed of East Coast Joint Stock paid for by all three East Coast partners, including the North British. There was also a contractual arrangement between NBR and NER — after 1904 the latter was effectively running all express trains on Edinburgh-Berwick section for a fee. In other words, the North British was in a hopelessly anomalous position regarding this contest, and must have welcomed its end. The company's own statistics for the arrival times of the racing 09.30 show an emphatic falling-off of performance from 9 July onwards, with a *total* of only one minute being saved on this train's passage over the Waverley Route in the whole of the rest of July. This is in contrast to 24min being saved in the first seven days on this most difficult of routes. (See also the accompanying table of arrival times.)

Table 7
The 'Placings', Railway Race, 1901

	July 1st	2nd	3rd	4th	5th	6th	8th
First	NE	NE	NE	NE	CR	CR	NB
Second	NB	NB	NB	NB	NE	NE	CR
Third	—	—	—	—	NB	NB	NE
Margin (Mins)	4	15	6	12	29	8	2

Interestingly, the gap between these trains was to narrow to only 5min by 1910, but by that time the NER's running powers over the NBR's Berwick-Edinburgh section were no longer a matter of contention between the companies. In 1901 they most certainly were, and the Midland and NBR's apparently innocent timetabling of their 09.30 was too provocative for the NER to bear.

Table 8
Arrival times of London-Edinburgh expresses at Edinburgh termini from 1-6 July, and on 8 July 1901

Arrival at	Waverley		Princes St
	GN/NE	M/NB	LNW/C
Scheduled at	18.15	18.05	18.15
Mon 1st	18.02	18.06	18.34
Tues 2nd	18.03	18.18	18.30
Wed 3rd	18.09	18.15	18.17
Thurs 4th	18.07	18.19	18.15
Fri 5th	18.09	18.12	17.40
Sat 6th	18.06	18.15	17.58
Mon 8th	18.09	18.05	18.07

Sources: *Railway Times/Scotsman.*

So ended an exciting but inconclusive episode in the history of Anglo-Scottish running. But it may have had one important seminal effect. The Midland turned to the concept of Train Control not long afterwards, doubtless realising the impracticability of 'pathing' high-speed, long-distance expresses among a network of, believe it or not, *untimetabled* coal trains. Its Scottish ally, the North British was not long in following its example — each company was the first in its own country to implement Train Control, something which has become an integral part of railway administration.

The NBR's first control room was situated at Portobello, less than a mile from the East junction, the 'finishing line' of the 1901 Race to the North.

Above:

Portobello East Junction looking towards Edinburgh with Class 55 No 55008 *The Green Howards*, already displaced from major London-Edinburgh expresses by IC125s, powering the 09.50 Waverley-Plymouth express on 19 September 1980. The South Leith branch is clearly visible in the background immediately to the left of the Class 37 diesel at the head of a Freightliner rake.

M. Macdonald

6
Edinburgh as a Locomotive Building Centre

Unlike its neighbour city, Glasgow, Edinburgh has never been an acknowledged centre for the building of railway locomotives. Yet a large number of steam locomotives have been outshopped by city builders in years now long gone, and at least one such engine still exists. Not only that, but only a quirk of fate prevented a Leith-built locomotive competing against the victorious *Rocket* in the Rainhill Locomotive Trials of 1829.

As mentioned in the section on locomotive depots, St Margaret's was the first locomotive-building centre for the North British Railway, 33 engines being constructed there between 1856 and 1869. The first of these were two 2-2-2T engines, Nos 31 and 32, designed for local passenger traffic, and the last to be outshopped was a 2-4-0 tender engine with 6ft diameter driving wheels. It lasted in service until 1912, none of Meadowbank's output surviving World War 1.

After 1869, it was natural that NBR locomotive construction should be concentrated on the former Edinburgh & Glasgow works at Cowlairs in Glasgow. St Margaret's continued to repair locomotives until 1925, but its constricted site was not conducive to heavy engineering operations, particularly while the Springburn area of Glasgow was fast building up a reputation as a prime site for steam engine construction, with an expert workforce.

But the NBR's was not the only locomotive

Below:
Edinburgh built! NBR 0-6-0 No 67A, photographed at an unknown location sometime between 1882, when this number was allocated, and 1895 when she was renumbered 848 and scrapped. Originally built at the Hawthorn Leslie Works beside the Water of Leith at Leith's Junction Street, this engine was rebuilt in the NB's own works at St Margaret's in 1869, the year that new construction ceased there. *C. Highet collection/SRO*

building operation in the city, and one Edinburgh veteran built as long ago as 1861 still survives. This is an industrial user 0-4-0WT with outside cylinders and a dome unusually mounted on the firebox. Named *Ellesmere*, and numbered 244, she was the product of Hawthorn Leslie of Leith. Brought back from the Wigan area by an enthusiast when her career was drawing to a close, No 244 had scarcely celebrated its centenary when she passed into the hands of the Scottish Railway Preservation Society, and is now owned by the Royal Museums of Scotland — not, it must unfortunately be said, the most inspired exhibitor of Scottish transport artefacts.

Better known as a Tyneside firm, Hawthorns had set up a subsidiary in Leith in 1846 to meet the Scottish demand for locomotives without having to ship completed engines up the coast at a time when the Tweed had still not been bridged by rail. The erection of completed parts in Leith was soon followed by construction from 'scratch', one of the first orders to be carried out at the Great Junction Street yard being motive power for the Edinburgh Leith & Granton Railway.

Around 1850 Hawthorns appear to have sold their Leith business, which nevertheless seems to have continued trading under their name. No fewer than 425 engines were outshopped at this site by the Water of Leith before 1872 (approximately where the State cinema/bingo hall is now), with operations continuing into the 1880s. As well as meeting the needs of a number of smaller Scottish railways, the Leith firm exported to India, Germany, South Africa and South America.

Locomotive building also seems to have been undertaken in the city by T. M. Tennant & Co, first in the Newington and St Leonard's districts, then at Bowershall Works, off Bonnington Road, in Leith from 1862. No details appear to be available of locomotives constructed at any of these sites, which may of course have included road and traction engines. Similarly, the listing of Leonard J. Todd of Leith as an engine builder in James W. Lowe's superb book *British Steam Locomotive Builders* probably implies some kind of steam tram for road purposes, and D. L. G. Hunter mentions in his highly-valuable book *Edinburgh's Transport* a Todd-built road vehicle plying between Leith and the West End in the 1870s, so this constructor can probably be discounted as a railway engineer.

More significant undoubtedly, is the inclusion of Timothy Burstall in the list of city locomotive builders. This Leith engineer is recorded in the postal directories of the time as working from 'Leith Mills', and more information about him would be highly interesting. In 1829 he entered a steam locomotive entitled *Perseverance* in the Rainhill trials, although it was unfortunately damaged in transit to Liverpool, and did not take part in the contest. That it would be unlikely to have given *Rocket* much competition is suggested by its description — a vertical boiler mounted on a four-wheel frame. The 57cwt machine could travel at around 3-4mph, but, lacking a separate condensing chamber, must have required a considerable amount of perseverance to operate!

Another 'home-made' industrial engine constructed in the capital was an overhead-collector electric engine built by Bruce Peebles Ltd for its own system in Edinburgh around 1903 and scrapped in 1961.

Perhaps not an impressive array of locomotives, compared with the output of the Glasgow and West of Scotland firms, but Edinburgh is not usually associated with locomotive construction at all, so these products of local firms are doubly interesting. In particular, it is fascinating to think that an Edinburgh engineer was preparing an entry in the 1829 Locomotive Trials, before a yard of track was open for traffic in the Scottish capital.

7
St Leonard's — The Capital's First Station

An undistinguished housing estate off the Pleasance is all that remains of the site of Edinburgh's first station. This was the St Leonard's terminus of the Edinburgh and Dalkeith Railway which reached the city in 1831.

The E&D was one of the country's first railways, intended to bring Lothian coal into the Scottish capital and to the ports of Leith and Fisherrow. Its network was almost X-shaped, centering on Niddrie. St Leonard's was the destination of one of the westward arms of this cross, the other being to South Leith. Eastwards, the arms reached out to Fisherrow, Musselburgh's port, and southeastwards towards Newtongrange in the Lothian coal-mining area.

Modern vestiges of this crucial railway layout are the South Leith goods branch — still busy with freight traffic, and recently integrated into new road developments in the Portobello area — and the old E&D embankment which can still be seen running along the south side of Baileyfield Road. Cyclists have reason to thank the former company for its line into St Leonard's from Craigmillar, as this is now an attractive cycle-way skirting the southern shore of Duddingston Loch bird-sanctuary. From the site of the 'Bonny Wells of Wearie' in Holyrood Park the line climbed at the fierce gradient of 1 in 30 through a gas-lit tunnel which still exists, emerging among the aforementioned houses in the formerly commercial surroundings of St Leonard's.

A contemporary description of the St Leonard's tunnel is worth examining, as this feature still exists in Edinburgh's Holyrood Park, its eastern portal directly beneath the rock formation known imaginatively as 'Samson's Ribs'. In 1840, Francis Whishaw recorded that the tunnel was 572yd long, with a 20ft bore and lit by 25 gas lamps. The incline was more than twice as long — 1,160yd — and here horse-power gave way to 'two low-pressure (stationary) condensing engines', with 28in cylinders, constructed by Carmichael of Dundee. These drove the cable round an 11ft-diameter drum which would haul up 30-ton loads at a time, totalling between 130 and 190 wagons daily, taking 5min on the journey. The E&D had even perfected 'a self-acting stopper', a device carried on the train to prevent a breakaway on the incline, by (rather alarmingly) ensuring an immediate derailment.

The E&D was known as the 'Innocent Railway' because of an apocryphal reputation for never having injured anyone. In fact staff accidents were frequent, as Whishaw records, and C. Hamilton Ellis is probably nearer the mark in ascribing the soubriquet to what one contemporary writer called its 'indestructive character'. It was laid to the old 'Scotch' gauge of 4ft 6in and was horse-powered. The company at first allowed non-company agents to organise passenger services, but took this facility over from about 1836 after discovering that passenger-carrying could be a lucrative activity — earning a revenue of £4,000 in 1842.

However, the E&D 'conductor-guards' encountered difficulties in persuading passengers to buy tickets; members of the public objected to telling 'ony speirin' loon' where they were going! In 1839, the line's manager David Rankine, when asked by a Parliamentary committee about the non-supply of tickets, replied 'We do not use them . . . we have always found that many persons would not tell, or did not make up their minds, where they were going, which causes great confusion . . .'

One passenger recalled that travelling on the E&D meant 'you can examine the crops as you go along; you have time to hear the news from your companions'. (Doesn't seem so bad really?) The company even had the initiative to organise a bathers' special at 06.00 from St Leonard's to Portobello, advertised by exhorting the Edinburgh public 'to be up betimes, treating themselves to a pleasant ride and a refreshing bath, instead of the false luxury of a snooze in bed'. There was a similar service on the EL&G out of Canal Street.

Innocent or not, the Edinburgh & Dalkeith appears to have been highly successful in everything it attempted. Historian John Thomas pointed out that its passenger-carrying operations per mile of track were superior to those of its pioneering Stockton & Darlington and Liverpool & Manchester contemporaries. But it was really in coal transport that it excelled, playing a major part in the doubling of the

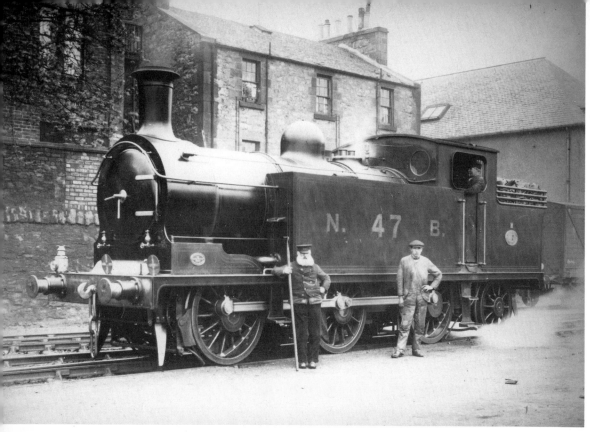

Above:
NBR 'N15/1' 0-6-2T No 47 poses with its crew and a splendidly bewhiskered shunter at St Leonard's probably immediately after World War 1. The fearsome gradient up to this terminus from Duddingston was even steeper than Glasgow's Cowlairs Incline, for which this 0-6-2T type (originally 'N14') was initially designed, and this locomotive was allowed to propel no more than 24 loaded wagons up the incline, having worked up as much momentum as possible on the level stretch past Duddingston Loch. *W. E. Boyd collection*

amount of coal supplied to Edinburgh and Leith in the first half of the 19th century. This is not surprising, considering it was the inspiration of a cartel of Lothian coal-mine owners who gave the railway's list of subscribers what C. J. A. Robertson has called 'an aristocratic flavour, being led by a duke, a marquis, two earls, a viscount and five baronets'. All this for what started off as a coal waggonway a few miles in length!

In 1845 the E&D was bought by the North British Railway which regauged the line and introduced steam locomotives. It quickly lost its separate identity within the NBR, but continued to play an important role in the Lothian transport network for many years. Part of the network — the southward spur towards Newtongrange — provided the NBR with a launching-point for its Hawick branch which eventually became the (now closed) Waverley Route

to Carlisle where traffic was exchanged with the Midland Railway. Diverging from the Waverley route, the E&D's Dalkeith branch gave the NBR a passenger terminus, in use for over a century until 1942. Its site is now the local bus station, confirming that the original railway operator knew a good passenger site when they saw one! The St Leonard's spur took on considerable importance in an area populated by brewing and bonding concerns, fulfilling a freight role until the late 1960s. As for the Leith branch, it still carries freight today, as will be seen when the port's rail facilities, past and present, are examined.

It is interesting that, whatever comparatively small contribution freight makes to BR's income in the Lothians, the old Edinburgh & Dalkeith Railway network has played a seminal role in ensuring its continuance. Edinburgh's only non-container rail freight centre (at South Leith), and the continuing existence of coal traffic into Leith, are evidence that this venerable company played an important part in Edinburgh's — and Scotland's — rail development.

As the modern reader imagines horse-drawn E&D trains trundling through the capital's environs, each guard equipped with a bugle which, one traveller of the time records, 'he sounds lustily as the occasion requires', the aptness of the nickname 'Innocent Railway' becomes apparent. The Edinburgh & Dalkeith was a product of the Industrial Revolution, and saw no reason why it should grow up.

8
Leith's Railways

Unlike St Leonard's, the station building of the 'other' Edinburgh & Dalkeith railway terminus in Edinburgh was until recently to be seen at South Leith just a few yards from the main dock gates at the north end of Constitution Street. Of course, when the station opened for passengers in 1838, Leith was not part of Edinburgh, but a separate burgh, a status it maintained legally until 1920.

As the Leith terminus of the E&D, South Leith was sited next to the waves of the Firth of Forth, and was so well placed for members of the Lothian coal community visiting the port that it survived the opening of Leith Central 65 years later. The development of the docks distanced the station from the sea in the latter part of the 19th century, but the branch from here to Portobello carries freight traffic to this day. Around the time of the station's closure to passengers on 2 January 1905 (effectively 31 December 1904), extensive yards were built next to the Seafield Road.

South Leith Goods Depot is in fact the only general freight loading/unloading point in the city, and was the busiest depot of its kind in Scotland in 1985, handling 55,584 tons of merchandise. A new distribution centre has been built here, rail-borne goods being transferred by road. Private enterprise supplied the necessary investment in replacing the only-recently demolished goods shed with a purpose-built centre.

One of the staple traffics dealt with is heavy-duty gas pipes which are coated in the Leith area and distributed nationwide by rail. Another is the 'import' of grain from East Anglia, now carried from the port in high-capacity Polybulk vehicles.

In the 1980s, coal was once again brought to the quayside at Leith by rail from the Blindwells open-cast site in East Lothian, only yards from the trackbed of Scotland's first waggonway between Tranent and the harbour of Cockenzie. Strange how these echoes of Scotland's industrial past continue to resound into our modern railway age! In particular it is ironic that the first railway into Edinburgh's port should also be its only remaining one. Interestingly, three other passenger termini in Leith have vanished from the railway map –

Below:
Despite the unplanned trackside flora, South Leith Yard represents a busy sight on 29 June 1984. On the left No 47226 has brought in ammonia tanks from Haverton Hill and these are being propelled on the right by No 08588 towards the SAI complex. In the middle, Class 20s Nos 20067/069 are about to take a similar cargo to Grangemouth. *M. Macdonald*

although by a curious coincidence, the remains of all four stations could still be seen in Leith until the late 1980s.

The town's second terminus to be built was situated at the Cromwellian Citadel at Commercial Street. This was the Edinburgh Leith & Granton's branch station in the port, opened in 1846, later to become the North British North Leith terminus. Its traffic reached the capital by way of the Scotland Street tunnel already mentioned, with the more modern Abbeyhill route opening in 1868. There were five intermediate stations, the first of these at Junction Road, right beside the Water of Leith, just through the tunnel from Citadel. Bonnington Road station building is still to be seen beside the present walkway which runs from Junction Street by the old (pre-Abbeyhill) route through Warriston to Heriot-hill. One platform at Bonnington is still adorned by a

Top:
Gresley 'V3' 2-6-2T No 67668 at the North British South Leith station on a rail tour in August 1962.
G. M. Staddon/N. E. Stead collection

Above:
St Margaret's 'J83' 0-6-0T No 68448 at South Leith in October 1953. The letters 'LGW' on the wagons denoted Leith General Warehousing, and the wagons ran from Leith Docks around the suburban lines to Haymarket Goods, and lasted to the early 1970s.
G. M. Staddon/N. E. Stead collection

Right:
Class V3 2-6-2T No 67624 approaching the former Bonnington station in May 1956. Off to the right was a spur which crossed the Water of Leith and served a sizeable goods depot at West Bowling Green Street. The main track bed now forms a part of the Water of Leith Walkway. *G. M. Staddon/N. E. Stead collection*

horseshoe mark – presumably indicating the use at one time of horse-drawn traffic from this point on to the nearby goods-only branch across the river and into the Bonnington goods yard. Powderhall was served by a station for a comparatively short time, now the site of the District Council siding for refuse trains, while Leith Walk had its own station on this line at Shrubhill, with Easter Road station sited farther east.

The North Leith branch line was a busy one – in 1903 the NBR found that the branch generated more passenger traffic than its new Central terminus (84,000 as against 70,000 tickets), Bonnington Road having the busiest turnover on the branch. The cramped layout of the terminus with its single platform close to the tunnel-mouth must have caused operational difficulties and not surprisingly, the LNER introduced steam railcar services on the line from about 1929, Leithers promptly dubbing each car with the nickname the 'Ghost'. Closure to passengers came in 1947 but some fish traffic continued on the line for another quarter-century, along with freight traffic to and from Bonnington.

The third Leith passenger terminus – and the last to close – was Leith (North), the former Caledonian station at Lindsay Road, just off North Junction Street. This interesting structure, which still exists largely intact, consisted of an island platform surmounted by a wooden train-shed. Its restricted layout meant that arriving trains had to propel themselves back out of the station, the locomotive coming off while the coaches' brakes were secured,

and the stock then allowed to roll back into the platform. Despite such operational handicaps, there is no evidence of any railcar operation on the Caledonian branch until the coming of DMUs in the later 1950s. The 1910 timetable showed an average of 21min for the journey to Princes Street, with stops at Newhaven, Granton Road, Craigleith, Murrayfield, and Dalry Road. A further stop was later added at East Pilton, near Crewe Toll in 1934.

Just before World War 2, the LMS was actually offering as many daily journeys between Edinburgh's city centre and its Leith station (not named 'North' until BR days) as the LNER was with its two Leith termini combined – 37 services as against 27 between Waverley and Leith Central and 11 to and from North Leith.

Closure came in April 1962, ironically with the last passenger trains terminating in the shadow of new high-rise flats which might have generated some additional railway business when completed shortly afterwards.

Besides services to the west end of Leith, the line offered the Caledonian a launching-pad for a new cross-Leith line from the Trinity area to Seafield. Announced in 1889, this would have been the northern arm of the company's planned circle for the north Edinburgh area, the Princes Street underground line providing the southern arm. The lines would have met near Lochend, where a triangular junction would have provided a branch to Seafield, just across Salamander Street from the North British's South Leith branch. Leith Town Council

Top:
LNER Sentinel railcar No 38 *Pearl* worked on the Stirling-Balloch service until its withdrawal in 1934, before being reallocated to St Margaret's to operate North Leith branch trains. According to Charles Meacher, these units had to be based at Leith Central, away from the depot itself, to protect the upholstery from grime and to deny railway night-shift workers the chance of an undetected nap! *Real Photos*

Above:
A Gloucester DMU stops at East Pilton on a Princes Street-Leith North local in April 1962. This halt served the Bruce Peebles engineering works, which can be seen behind the train. This former railway is now a walkway. *G. M. Staddon/N. E. Stead collection*

Top right:
Caledonian '3F' 0-6-0 No 57559 approaches Craigleith station with the 13.43 from Leith North in April 1958. The branch to the left went to Davidson's Mains and Barnton. Walkways now follow the rail routes.
G. M. Staddon/N. E. Stead collection

Centre right:
Craigleith station in August 1955 with Dalry Road '2P' 0-4-4T No 55202 on the 13.43 from Leith North to Princes Street. The Crest Hotel is now behind the trees on the right. *G. M. Staddon/N. E. Stead collection*

Right:
The remains of a late fall of snow line the platform edge at Murrayfield station in March 1957 as '2P' 0-4-4T No 55229 enters with a local train bound from Leith North to Princes Street.
G. M. Staddon/N. E. Stead collection

Top:
Granton Road station, on the Princes Street-Leith North branch, as seen in 1934. Some gardening is under way on the down platform; there is little indication that the Leith branch enjoyed some 38 trains per day in each direction at this period. *Real Photos*

Above:
Newhaven station, the last stop before the terminus on the Princes Street-North Leith branch. It is seen here on a summer day in 1932, looking westwards. To the left of the picture is the cutting which would have carried the connection from the Leith (CR) terminus along the company's New Leith Lines to Seafield or Leith East. Unlike the Edinburgh-facing connection on the west side of Newhaven, no track was ever laid here. The goods lines on the right of the picture lead beyond the photographer to Leith Docks and George Street Goods Depot. Not a yard of this rail scene still exists.
Real Photos

Above right:
North Leith was the Leith terminus of the Edinburgh Leith and Newhaven branch from Canal Street via Scotland Street (until 1868) and then from Waverley via Abbeyhill (until branch closure in 1947). Despite the austere appearance of the station, seen here without its overall roof and loop in August 1964, the branch was busy with passenger traffic and even had a daily departure for Glasgow (Queen Street) before the opening of Leith Central. The LNER used Sentinel steam railcars on the line, but the city's trams and buses offered passengers a service into and out of the city centre without the spectre of the climb out of Waverley. *Real Photos*

Right:
The simple train shed at Leith North in April 1962, and Driver F. Minay poses beside his Gloucester DMU, about to depart for Princes Street.
G. M. Staddon/N. E. Stead collection

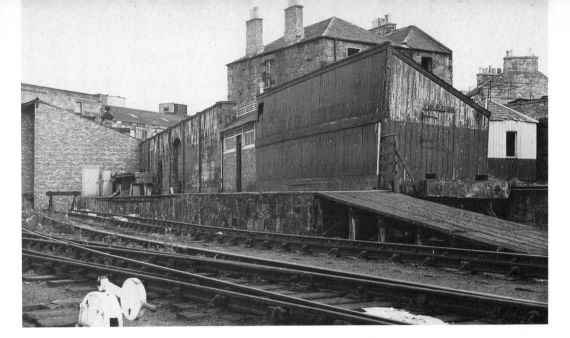

asked for no fewer than seven intermediate stations
to be built, and the Caledonian promised never to
charge more than its rival company for passenger
trips to and from central Edinburgh.

It was a bold concept, doomed almost immediately
to failure in Parliament thanks to the NBR's promise
of a short branch from Abbeyhill to the foot of Leith
Walk (ie to what became Leith Central). This could
be built without any disruption to Princes Street, so
the Caledonian's eastern approach to Leith failed.
Perhaps it was just as well – with the NBR later
charging only a penny for single journeys to or from
Leith Central, the ambitious underground Caledonian line, running under Princes Street and
burrowing through the volcanic rock of the Calton
Hill, was hardly likely to have recovered its costs
with its fares pinned to the NBR level. As it was, the
'Caley' was committed to building the line eastwards from Trinity to Seafield, and this was
expensive enough.

Never open to passenger traffic after its completion in August 1903, and closed altogether since
1968, this cross-Leith line was elevated for much of
its length. Its bridges were landmarks in the port,
particularly those spanning Leith Walk and Bonnington Road, bringing a Glasgow-like atmosphere
to the townscape. Three stations began construction

– near Craighall Road, under Ferry Road and above
Manderston Street, this last just off the Walk and
within sight of the North British's new terminus of
Leith Central.

The Seafield terminus remained as a freight depot
only, and as far as is known, the only passenger
trains to traverse the line were the very occasional
special working. There was a fair amount of traffic
to and from the South Leith area, while Leith Walk
goods stations (not to be confused with the former
NBR establishment on the North Leith/Granton
branch) remained open until the end. The 'Caley'
does not appear to have considered this depot as a
possible passenger terminus for Leith despite its
location being superior to Seafield. The NBR took
over the Caledonian shed at Seafield during World
War 1 to service its own Leith operations and there
was a later informal arrangement that traffic on the
former Caledonian line would be worked by
St Margaret's during BR days.

So ended a bold (perhaps over-bold) and expensive
bid by the Glasgow-based Caledonian to establish
itself in Leith, then one of Scotland's busiest ports.
Few vestiges of the line remain in the area, although
the trackbed from Hawkhill down to Seafield is now
a walkway, and the intended Leith Walk station site
still exists on the roof of what used to be the Capitol
cinema.

Leith Central – the station nobody wanted

Only recently demolished, Leith Central was Edinburgh's third largest station, one of the top 12 in Scotland, and may have held the record of being Britain's biggest terminus built from scratch in the 20th century. Yet its closure was not even mentioned in the local newspapers in 1952, and, when asked in 1985, British Rail Property Board were unable to say to whom they had disposed of it (actually Edinburgh District Council). They did confirm that the station was Scotland's biggest closed station still substantially complete, so even after closure the Central continued to break records.

Occupying the whole length of Duke Street, the terminus was bounded by Leith Walk on the west side and by Easter Road appropriately on the east. Its impact on the passer-by, particularly in Leith Walk, was lessened by what the Penguin *Buildings of Scotland* guide describes as 'weak Renaissance frontages'. These included shops and pubs at ground-level, one of the latter being notable for its tiled sporting scenes, while from the first floor, Leith Walk was overlooked by waiting-rooms and office accommodation. A three-faced tower clock still beams down on Leithers from the corner of the Walk and Duke Street, and below this the main staircase entrance was sited. There was a subway entrance at the Easter Road end, where some 4,500sq ft of accommodation was available under the tracks at street level. The carriageway, the most imposing of the three entrances, made a brave sweep up from Leith Walk to the site of the former internal cab-rank.

With buffer-stops situated at the western end, the Central had a concourse giving on to two island platforms with four faces, each approximately 790ft long, and numbered 1 to 4 from the south. Even the small loading space on the north side had an edge of about 120ft, although it was not a numbered platform. Twelve tracks wide at one point, the structure was topped by an Arrol steel-framed glass-panel roof some 13 sections in length, its width varying from 150ft at the western end and 220ft in the middle, to about 90ft above the platform ends, supported by coursed-rubble side walls with no internal pillars. Without its platforms in its final years, the abandoned building had more the atmosphere of an aircraft hangar than a railway station. The layout was completed by an 81-lever signalbox and a 51ft turntable west and east of Easter Road respectively.

Its extraordinary history can only be summarised here. Constructed without its own Act of Parliament, the Central was the price the NBR had to pay to obstruct the Caledonian's ambitious plan for an underground line running to Leith via Princes Street (thus threatening Waverley) and by tunnel through the Calton Hill. The NBR's offer of a line to the foot of the Walk from London Road Junction barely two miles away was the obvious solution to the local transport controversy of the time, and was popular with Leith Town Council, even if they would have preferred a joint NBR/CR station.

Unfortunately, the North British was convinced from the outset that the line would not be viable, and grudgingly opened the terminus in July 1903, offering trains half-hourly to Waverley only, and with a minimum of publicity, its limited number of entrances unmarked. Not surprisingly, when a local minister, the Reverend Crerar, attempted to catch

77

one of the first trains at the Central, he stumbled into a pub by mistake!

The gloomy view of the Central held by its owners only deepens the mystery as to why it was so big. We know that the Leith burgh councillors and officials were astonished by its size when given their first sight of the station plans – although it did not stop them requesting the addition of the corner clock-tower. Carriage-storage was always one of the station's functions, pre-dating the construction of Craigentinny sidings by some 10 years, but the NBR was hardly likely to build such an expensive edifice for the storing of empty stock! One historian believes that the NBR may have anticipated a huge growth in USA-bound emigrant traffic from the Baltic, through Leith to the West Coast ports, but, whatever the reason for its size, the Central was always too big for its traffic.

At the time of its opening a local newspaper imaginatively described the new terminus with its inaugural train, headed by a diminutive tank engine, as a 'four-storey kennel for a Skye terrier pup'. Indeed, when a serious fire broke out in October 1937, destroying one of the two major island platforms, some rail vehicles, and asphyxiating countless pigeons, the next day's passenger services were quite unaffected, so great was the station's over-capacity.

Besides services to Waverley, the company offered departures round the Southside suburban circle, linking Leith with Morningside in only 21min, and Waverley within seven, including the Abbeyhill stop. Some Glasgow trains left and terminated from here,

their steam locomotives hardly being helped by having to toil up the 1 in 62 through Lochend before attempting a fast schedule westwards from Waverley.

Helped by the 'Pilrig Muddle' – the chaos created by the fact that Leith's electric tramway met Edinburgh's incompatible cable tramway at the Burgh boundary, requiring through passengers to change trams – the Central surprised the NBR with its heavy traffic initially. Indeed, the archival papers relating to this almost-forgotten station contain a letter from an enterprising workman named Smith, who, in 1920, suggested to the NBR that they were losing potential suburban traffic by not laying on a scheduled service for the many Leith artisans who travelled to Gorgie (on the Suburban Circle) for factory employment. Apparently, Mr Smith and his colleagues were in the habit of avoiding the 'Muddle' by walking to Pilrig and there taking an Edinburgh tram to their destination. The only problem was – they were compelled to travel 'outside' the car, ie on the open upper deck exposed to the elements. As he informed the NB, 'The railway is losing workmen's money that the cars do not deserve to get'. The company, already shown to be strangers to the concept of market research by their failure to realise their advantages over the local tram services between Leith and Edinburgh, took Smith's letter very seriously. The result was a 07.16 service from Central to Blackford Hill, arriving at a convenient time at Gorgie before eight o'clock. Its only drawback was a 15min dead stand at Waverley, although at least the passengers kept dry!

However, after 1922, when Edinburgh and Leith tram systems were unified and came into their own, and the 'Pilrig Muddle' was no more, the Central lost traffic and closed in 1952, less than 50 years after opening – probably a record for a custom-built station of such size.

It later served as Scotland's first diesel mainten-ance depot and driving school until 1972. During this period its length proved invaluable for providing under-cover facilities for storing and servicing the six-coach Swindon-built 'InterCity' DMUs introduced on the Waverley-Glasgow (Queen Street) run in January 1957. Former driver Charles Meacher recalls that, as fuel gauges were regarded as unreliable in early diesel days on BR, fuel tanks were allowed to fill to overflowing at the Central to prevent shortages 'on the road'. What this did for the smell and fire safety conditions in the former station, to say nothing for its foundations and those of surrounding tenements, can only be guessed at.

It seems incredible now that express trains headed by streamlined A4 Pacifics, or even 'P2' 2-8-2s such as *Cock o' the North,* were once to be seen here, only yards from the shoppers and pedestrians in one of Edinburgh's most important thoroughfares.

Above:
Leith Central, once a record-breaking railway terminus, was one of the biggest stations built from scratch in Britain in the 20th century and had a working life of less than 50 years, surely a record for a station of such a size. It is pictured here in April 1987, looking westwards, attended by the formerly 81-lever frame signalbox and cut off from the photographer by the removal of Easter Road bridge. The whole structure was demolished in 1989. *Author*

9
Lothian Lines

Mention has been made in the introductory chapters of the Lothian Lines, and a more lengthy description of them is perhaps appropriate. Or is it? Nowadays little remains of this network of goods-only lines, at least south of Portobello. Yet, they are surely worthy of some study, particularly since their primary function — the transport of coal — is not moribund, even in the reduced freight-carrying patterns of the present Edinburgh rail network.

To begin with, the Lothian Lines represented a fairly unusual example of a railway company creating an almost-microcosmic rail network on, and *in addition* to, its existing infrastructure of lines. Not only that, but they were the product of a company acting under direct commercial duress, and a reaffirmation of the traditional staple trade of coal movements in the Lothians. While it is true that nearly all the Lothian Lines are no longer in existence, the South Leith-Portobello section is still in use, and in the 1980s began to be used again for the transporting of Lothian-produced coal for export, or for shipping to London for electricity-generation.

In the 10 years before 1913 coal production in Mid and East Lothian was booming, increasing from 1.83 million tons to 4.06 million tons in that period. Nearly 70% of this was exported, almost all through Leith. According to statistics issued by the Lothian coalmasters, there was an approximate 300% increase in exported coal from the Lothians in the years 1904-12 alone. This was despite the fact that

Below:
Joppa station in August 1957, and NBR Class N15 No 69146 prepares to use the crossover; note the disc ground signal, controlled from the signalbox between the footbridge and the stone road bridge. The Joppa platforms have now vanished from the ECML although this station building still exists on the down side. The bridge supports in the left background carry the Lothian Lines between Portobello and Leith, and the chimney is that of the railway laundry.
G. M. Staddon/N. E. Stead collection

Class N15 0-6-2T No 69135 on the Lothian Lines from Niddrie North in June 1959. The parallel tracks are the suburban lines to Portobello. The tender of a 'J37' is just visible through the bridge on the right, and is on the direct line to Monktonhall. To the right of this are lines to Millerhill. *G. M. Staddon/N. E. Stead collection*

Left:

Elderly North British 'Y9' 0-4-0T No 68119 shunts at the United Glass Bottle works at Portobello in May 1959. The letters 'SA' on the smokebox door denote 'spark arrester' which is not fitted on this occasion.
G. M. Staddon/N. E. Stead collection

Below right:

A Glasgow Fair holiday special to Dunbar steams towards Joppa station in July 1960, hauled by Ivatt Class 4MT No 43133. It has just passed under the bridge carrying the single line between Portobello and Niddrie. The bridge has disappeared, and at this point the recently-built Portobello bypass road crosses the ECML. *G. M. Staddon/N. E. Stead collection*

Lothian coalmasters paid more than, for example, their Fife rivals, to transport their product to the quay — 1/2d (about 6p) per ton per mile over a rated 4.05 mile distance. The Fife owners were moving coal over a shorter distance to the sea in most cases, and there was a tradition in Fife for independent colliery railways running to the Forth — as at Charlestown, Fordell, and latterly, at Wemyss, the last being built in controversial circumstances, as John Thomas records.

In contrast, the Lothian pits found their product hampered by what they considered the NBR's inefficiency. In particular, the single-line nature of the South Leith-Portobello section was a chronic bottleneck, the 1 in 69 down to the sea past Baileyfield being a huge obstacle for the smooth passage of trains. Traction problems on the gradient in the up direction could easily be encountered even when empties were being hauled, while 'down' trains had to have their brakes pinned down manually on each individual wagon to prevent possible runaways. Understandably, trains travelling down the incline towards the sea occupied the section even longer than those toiling up the grade.

Withdrawal of passenger services on the single-line around 1904/05 enabled doubling to be carried out by Christmas 1912, considerably easing the problem. Even so, the company found that its coal-producing customers were still not satisfied with this slow progress in improvements and in 1912 the coal companies presented to Parliament their own scheme for a rail-link between the port of Leith and a number of pits — the Lothians Railway Bill. This was formulated on behalf of the Edinburgh, Lothian, and Dalkeith Colliery Companies, as well as a number of smaller coal concerns and the Summerlea Iron Co. The NBR was intelligent enough to 'pick off' individual companies by offering better terms on a discriminatory basis, and one of them, the Niddrie & Benhar Co, soon made its peace with its rail carrier.

The independent Lothian Railways scheme seems to have failed to pass the Lords when the NBR pledged to improve its services on offer. Interestingly, the now-abandoned scheme had involved the prospect of an embankment (in the sea!) from the Edinburgh Dock at Leith, breaking the shore-line at Seafield and crossing NBR tracks twice before reaching the Craigentinny area. The actual Lothian Lines as built by the NBR were not quite so gradiose, but were still a substantial addition to the capital's rail network, and were opened to traffic on 26 September 1915 using special signalling arrangements.

From the former E&D Line from Leith through Seafield, the new lines climbed steeply to the main line a few yards to the north of Portobello station, where there was a junction into the goods yards, before swinging up a steeply-graded single-line above the town and curving southwards across both East Coast and Waverley Routes (which divided nearby at Portobello East junction) to approach Niddrie North. Here, the freight lines split three ways — westwards to join the Suburban circle line thus giving Leith traffic a route to the west and north avoiding reversal at Portobello, southwards to join the Waverley Route and its associated branches, and east to Wanton Walls, and ultimately to the East Coast main line at Monktonhall Junction.

So skilfully woven were the Lothian Lines into the existing railway infrastructure, that the single line running above the town of Portobello could carry coal traffic from Tranent, Macmerry, Newtongrange, the Polton, Penicuik and Loanhead branches, as well as Niddrie, West Lothian or Fife. Not surprisingly, it was intensively used in steam days, Portobello citizens nightly being entertained to locomotive pyrotechnics as NBR 0-6-0s toiled up the bank within earshot of every part of the town. The Portobello bypass road follows this route and, in truth, can hardly be noisier than what it has replaced.

In 1913 the North British gained a Scottish 'first' when it opened the first Train Control centre north of the Border at Portobello. Its construction was inextricably linked with the planning of the Lothian Lines and proved an immediate success, despite an early lack of telephone wire to complete its facilities. In September 1913, Superintendent Black minuted General Manager Jackson that 'the system is fast realising in a large degree all the benefits that were expected from it'. In particular, he stressed that the railway's coal customers were impressed with the improvement in the service. The North British had, albeit slowly and under direct threat of commercial competition, headed off a surprising challenge to its supremacy of the Lothian heartlands.

As recorded in the section on South Leith FLD, coal is still to be seen being moved around Midlothian by rail.

10
Edinburgh's Depots

Nowadays, with maintenance or servicing depots existing in Edinburgh only at Haymarket, Millerhill, and — for electric locomotives — at Craigentinny, it is easy to forget the former variety of locomotive centres in the city, St Margaret's, Dalry Road, Leith Central and Seafield, were important depots as well as Haymarket, and there were small sub-sheds at St Leonard's, Musselburgh, and South Leith, the last having no building. If the former EL&G Heriothill workshops are included, this all adds up to a fascinating collection of sites where engines were shedded and maintained.

St Margaret's

Listed in BR steam days as 64A, St Margaret's was the city's biggest now-vanished engine shed. Not a brick now stands of this once-notorious depot, most of whose site is occupied by office accommodation in the Jock's Lodge/Meadowbank area. The running shed, ash disposal lye, turntable and coaling stage (this last a manually-operated system) were all squeezed into a triangular space between the East Coast main line and the A1 road. Here at one time up to 221 steam locomotives had to be serviced by a maximum of 1,500 men in what former city engineman Charles Meacher describes 'an ill-

planned and badly-sited inheritance from the early 19th century'.

The original running-shed was a roundhouse on the north (up) side of the ECML, with covered carriage sidings on the other side. It was on to the latter site that the engine sheds 'overflowed', possibly after the E&G's carriage sidings on the west of the city became available in the 1860s. A six-road shed was soon built, followed later by a smaller, shorter one, built specially for North Eastern engines, and paid for by that company.

This was a result of the 1869 agreement for NER locomotives to power the major Anglo-Scottish trains on the ECML between Edinburgh and Newcastle, even although the metals north of Berwick-on-Tweed were North British owned and maintained. This smaller building was completed in 1871 at a cost of nearly £10,000, but North Eastern historian Ken Hoole records that the North British immediately cast envious eyes on the underused accommodation available to its southern partner! Not surprisingly, an agreement was made for NBR engines to share the space, with appropriate financial adjustment. This seemed to work well for around 30 years, when relations between NBR and NER were severely strained in the period before the signing of the 1904 agreement between the com-

Above:
NBR 'E' class 0-6-0 survived until 1932 as LNER 'J31'
No 10166, and was a permanent member of the
St Margaret's stud of freight engines. Locomotive
historians have noted that she was one of the last NBR
engines to retain 'quadruple slide bars and cottered big
ends' but non-specialists will note that she underwent
two major rebuildings without acquiring a cab for the
comfort of her crew! *Real Photos*

Right:
Originally numbered 111 and named *Clackmannan*,
LNER 'D51' No 10406 was one of a class of NBR 4-4-0
tanks which operated the company's light passenger
trains, often far from the area after which they were
named. This engine is seen at St Margaret's in 1931 two
years before her withdrawal, after some 53 years'
service. *Real Photos*

Below right:
W. P. Reid's 'C16' 4-4-2Ts were a common sight on
suburban passenger services in the Edinburgh area for
many years. This engine, No 9511 (BR 67497) is pictured
at St Margaret's where it was to end its career as a
stationary boiler after no fewer than 23 years
outshedded at Dunbar and Penicuik. No 9511's
retention of her smokebox wingplates is a splendid
period touch. *Real Photos*

Left:
Past St Margaret's, Thompson 'B1' class 4-6-0 No 61244
Strang Steel heads a semi-fast for Waverley in July
1953. *Brian Morrison*

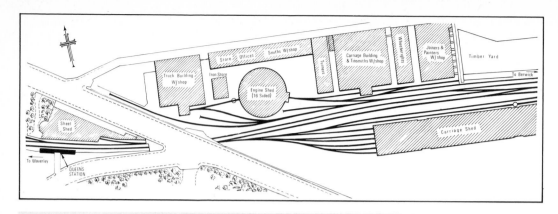

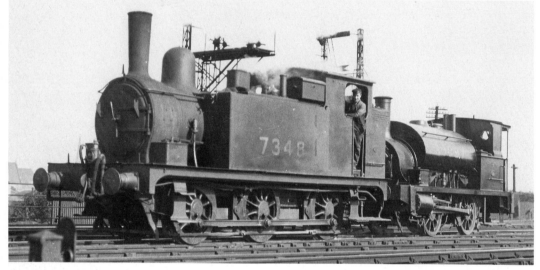

Top:
St Margaret's depot 1852.

Above:
A 1931 shot of former Great Eastern 'J69' No 7348 and 'Y9' No 10097 (the latter without its wooden tender), running from South Leith to St Margaret's after ascending from the shore-level and reversing at Portobello. *Real Photos*

panies. After that time, with the NER having almost unrestricted running powers over the North British's line north from Berwick-on-Tweed, NER green was seen at Haymarket instead of St Margaret's. The subsidiary shed appears to have been removed during reorganisation of the depot's south side during World War 2, when a 70ft vacuum turntable was installed, its site blasted from solid lava next to, and almost beneath, the Great North Road.

To reach the other (northern) side of the main line, railway staff had to cross the ECML at track level, sometimes unfortunately with fatal results, at a point where there was a nasty 'dog's-leg' curve in the ECML, just before northbound trains tackled 1¼ miles of 1 in 78 up to the Waverley platform-ends. The northern side of the depot once housed the original works of the North British Railway where some 33 locomotives were constructed before Cowlairs in Glasgow became the main locomotive-building centre for the company. (See Chapter 6.)

The original circular roundhouse was sited here until the roof was later destroyed by fire in the 1930s. This area used to be exclusively populated by tank engines, including Y9 dock tank, No 68095. This humble 0-4-0 locomotive may hold an all-comers' record for longevity of allocation to a single depot — a mere 80 years! Happily, it is now preserved, in Lancashire, far from the St Margaret's depot it called home for so long. (In actual fact, No 68095 and her sisters spent much of their time operating from South Leith depot, a St Margaret's sub-shed.)

St Margaret's depot was at one time responsible for running expresses to Carlisle over the Waverley Route, but the lack of regular rosters on the ECML restricted the shed's reputation for top-link work.

84

Such rostering lessened progressively with the passing of time seeing a substantial increase in the length of express passenger locomotives, which Haymarket was able to handle with greater convenience. The latter shed's most famous driver, Norman McKillop, mentions in his writings that St Margaret's gradually lost its more 'glamorous' turns; in contrast, it was responsible for nearly all of Midlothian's goods traffic, operating these through a series of sub-sheds, which in BR days at least, stretched as far as Galashiels, or Dunbar, up to 30 miles away.

The St Margaret's shed allocations for 1937 and 1959 are compared at the rear of this book. As if to confirm McKillop's words, it is noticeable that the 1937 locomotive complement of the single 'C10' Atlantic (there had been three only five years previously), the 'D11s', and the 'D49s' were used on Waverley Route expresses, only to be later replaced by 'V2s' and 'B1s', which had mixed traffic duties. By 1945 the shed's Top Link consisted of only five crews, all the drivers boasting at least 47 years of footplate experience.

An interesting byway in the history of St Margaret's concerns its Works library, one of only two in the NBR system, the other being at Cowlairs. The St Margaret's collection was instituted by the staff themselves in 1857 and maintained by a quarterly subscription of 6d (2½p). Its stock comprised fiction (Scott, Hugo, Dickens) books of exploration and adventure, but surprisingly few of a technical nature, although a number of engineering magazines were subscribed to. One of the library's strictest rules was that readers, not surprisingly, had to wash their hands before consulting books!

However, it seems that by the turn of the century the Librarian (honorarium £1 per annum) found it necessary to appeal to the NBR for financial support. He was requested to plead his case in front of the company's officials but was unable to do so, having

Above:
As a major rail centre Edinburgh has always had to provide emergency services to nearby areas, and here at Galashiels, some 30 miles down the Waverley Route from St Margaret's, that depot's crane comes to the assistance of a 'J36' off the track. This picture was taken in LNER days, and the entire Waverley Route was closed in 1969. *Real Photos*

Right:
Class J88 0-6-0T No 68338 with 'British Railways' lettering, on the turntable in May 1952, showing the tenements that dominated the St Margaret's site.
Brian Morrison

just undergone oral surgery. In the event, the General Manager and Superintendent of the Line thought the scheme worthy of support, and two guineas (£2.10) was granted annually from 1903, although only on application. A useful donation was also received from one of the Directors but more helpfully, a mention of the two libraries in the company's Weekly Notices led to a flood of new subscribers. By mid-Edwardian times there were over 100 St Margaret's library readers, the figure declining to around 50 by the advent of World War 1.

Such a site for steam locomotive maintenance, within a few yards of much tenemental housing, was not conducive to public health and BR was glad to dispose of it following closure in April 1967. Towards the end of its life the arrival of main line diesels at Haymarket had meant the transfer of Pacifics to 64A, their length doing nothing to ease the congestion problems.

Top:

No longer sporting her Royal Stewart tartan, old North British single-wheeler No 55 was originally a Crampton 4-2-0 delivered to the line in 1849 and was used to haul Queen Victoria's train from Berwick to Meadowbank (for Holyrood Palace) the following year. No 55 was rebuilt no fewer than three times, in 1853, 1867, and 1897. She was renumbered 55A in 1894, thus dating this photograph before that date, and withdrawn in 1909. *Real Photos*

Above:

Thomas Wheatley's first express passenger locomotive for the North British Railway was this 2-2-2 No 36, outshopped in 1867 and virtually a complete rebuild of a Hawthorn locomotive built in 1847. She is seen at the old E&G Haymarket depot, east of the present 'Sprinter' depot, some time in the 1880s. *Real Photos*

Apart from the William Younger Centre and the Meadowbank velodrome, which stand on the northern part of the depot site, there are two office blocks on the southern triangular area. Railway enthusiast travellers would never know, from the present-day nondescript townscape, that they were passing a former depot as their IC225 sweeps past at 85mph.

Haymarket

Haymarket depot still exists, although much changed from the days of steam. No longer dominated by the LNER concrete mechanised coaling-plant which loaded a locomotive tender by inverting a coal wagon above it, the open-ended running-shed was considered the major NBR depot in the city. Before Grouping in 1923, Haymarket supplied most of the passenger traction power for trains to the north and west, while NER engines enjoyed rented accommodation here after 1901 (at £25 pa, per engine).

The present 'Sprinter' depot location is in fact the second siting of Haymarket depot. Its first, when it supplied motive power for the Edinburgh & Glasgow's trains, was just to the west of Haymarket station, opposite the present-day Duff Street connection which allows Waverley's trains to directly reach the former Caledonian system. (Incidentally, archival maps show a Caledonian connection into the southern Haymarket platform — then a terminal bay — up to 1894, well before the present connection was ever heard of.)

Below:
Haymarket depot 1912.

Following the opening of the Forth Bridge, the NBR rebuilt the depot in its present location, complete with eight-road double-ended running shed, turntable and coaling-bank. It shedded its first engines in 1894, around the time that the lines between Waverley and Saughton were being doubled. This relocation explains why the depot is named 'Haymarket', although Roseburn or Murrayfield would be geographically more accurate; indeed, the present-day 'Sprinter' depot's fuel-tanks can be glimpsed in the background during televised international rugby matches from the adjacent Murrayfield stadium!

Following the Grouping of 1923, Haymarket began to come into its own as a depot almost exclusively operating express passenger turns — to the extent that, even at the height of World War 2, it had only two freight tender engines (both 'J36s') allocated there. By 1946 the shed was responsible for some two dozen freight turns, but mainly used 'K3s', 'O6s' (a type later rarely seen in the city), and 'V2s' visiting from Heaton or St Margaret's. In contrast, bigger and ever more glamorous express locomotives were to become fixtures at 64B, its later BR shed-code.

In 1924 some of the first LNER 'A1s' (later classed as 'A3s') were allocated to Haymarket starting with No 2563 *William Whitelaw* (renamed *Tagalie* in 1941), and local enginemen, at the suggestion of General Manager Sir Ralph Wedgwood, were allocated workings south of Berwick, and after 1928, south almost to York. They quickly began to forge a reputation for high-speed running on the lines south to Newcastle and (to a lesser extent) Carlisle which earned them the epithet 'Enginemen Elite'.

This was the title of the autobiography, published

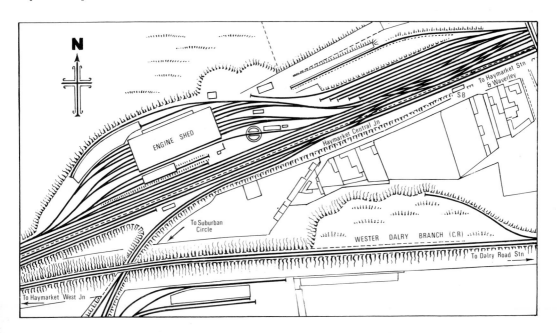

Top:
Former NBR motive power is outnumbered in this September 1925 shot of the western end of the Haymarket running-shed. On the left are 'J88' No 9844 and 'N14' No 9863, while the two more prominent English denizens are former North Eastern 'C7' Atlantic No 2194, and LNER (to a Great Central design) 'D11' 4-4-0 No 6381 *Flora MacIvor*, with former Great Northern 'D1' 4-4-0s Nos 3064 and 3065 also visible.
W. E. Boyd collection

Above:
Regarded by many railway enthusiasts as one of the finest Scottish designs ever produced, the Reid-designed NBR Atlantics certainly had a distinctive appearance. This is No 875 *Midlothian* photographed at Haymarket some time before December 1920, when this engine was superheated. *Real Photos*

Below:
Haymarket depot was the home of 'D30' 4-4-0 No 9411 *Dominie Sampson* in 1931 when this picture was taken. The NBR policy of naming engines after Sir Walter Scott's characters was an inventive one, and was continued in postwar days with the names given to Peppercorn's A1 Pacifics. Note that the NBR, for all its comprehensive naming policy, did not trouble with the expense of nameplates! *Real Photos*

Bottom:
2001 was the number of Gresley's magnificent 'P2' 2-8-2 *Cock o' the North,* and almost futuristic were the lines of this engine, photographed just a month after entering service from Haymarket depot in August 1934. Intended for working on the difficult Edinburgh-Aberdeen line, she and her sisters were rebuilt as 'A2' Pacifics by Edward Thompson in the 1940s, and reallocated south. *W. E. Boyd collection*

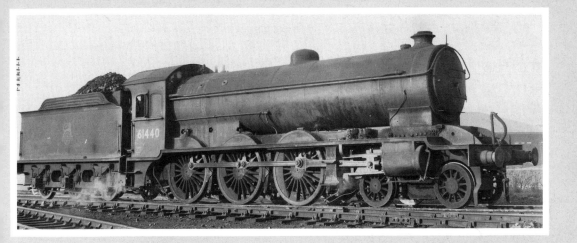

Above left:
NER Atlantics were commonplace in Edinburgh for the best part of 40 years, three or four of them being based at Haymarket. One which was not was NER Class 4CC No 730 (later classified as 'C8' by the LNER), working regularly into the city from Gateshead. This was a four-cylinder compound to the design of W. M. Smith, although Wilson Worsdell was the company's CME at the time of construction in 1906. Only two such engines were built, and this one, pictured reversing at Gorgie in August 1926 was borrowed by the NBR in 1908 to run trials against a Reid Atlantic on the Waverley Route. Unfortunately No 730 slipped so badly at Hawick that she was damaged and withdrawn from the trials. Nevertheless it is believed that only patenting problems prevented more of the class being constructed after Smith's death. *W. E. Boyd collection*

Left:
Pacific power at the east end of Haymarket shed around 1932. From left to right are 'A3s' Nos 2596

Manna, 2573 *Harvester,* 2563 *William Whitelaw* and a Raven 'A2' Pacific No 2402 *City of York.* *Real Photos*

Top:
Posing in the afternoon sunshine at Haymarket depot on 26 November 1955, is 'B16' 4-6-0 No 61440. The sight of the Murrayfield rugby grandstand in the right background emphasises how far Haymarket depot actually is from the station (and district) of the same name, having been rebuilt westwards of its original site by the NBR in 1894. *J. Robertson*

Above:
An Edinburgh engine for all of its 31 years, 'A3' No 60041 *Salmon Trout* is pictured at Haymarket, its home from 1934 to 1960, with a Class 40 diesel behind. This Pacific received its double chimney in 1959 but its 'elephant's ears' smoke deflectors were not fitted until January 1963, by which time *Salmon Trout* had crossed the city to St Margaret's, her final base. *Real Photos*

Below:
Haymarket express motive power old and new in 1925. About to set off from the depot on 30 June of that year for the Stockton & Darlington Centenary celebrations are Gresley 'A1' Pacific No 2563 *William Whitelaw* (the name being transferred to an 'A4' in 1941, when this engine was renamed *Tagalie*), and Reid Atlantic No 9902 *Highland Chief.* *W. E. Boyd collection*

Bottom:
When Gresley inherited a serious engine shortage on the NBR in the early 1920s his immediate reaction, apart from drafting in former Great Northern 'D1s', was to build examples of Robinson's Great Central 'Director'

4-4-0s of the 'D11' class. Here No 62692 *Allan-Bane* is seen at Haymarket in June 1957. *Brian Morrison*

Right:
One of the North British Class J36 0-6-0s which carried painted names – No 65235 *Gough* at Haymarket in June 1957. Sister engine *Maude* is preserved as NBR 673 by the SRPS. *Brian Morrison*

Bottom right:
Haymarket TMD in May 1988 with Class 107 DMU set No 107428 and Class 08 0-6-0 shunter No 08720 on view. *Brian Morrison*

by Ian Allan in 1958, of one Haymarket driver, the late Norman McKillop, whose championing of the Gresley Pacifics, particularly his own 'A3' No 60100 *Spearmint* made him one of the most entertaining railway writers of his time. Haymarket was regarded by some observers as the only depot on the East Coast route capable of challenging the King's Cross accolade of 'Top Shed', and the Edinburgh Pacifics were invariably cleaner, better maintained, and more skilfully driven than any other depot's. Haymarket came to be known as a 'Gresley' shed, and most histories of LNER motive-power mention (perhaps apocryphally) the indecent haste with which Haymarket, after the great designer's death, returned Edward Thompson's rebuild of the original 'A1' Pacific *Great Northern* to the south. And why should Haymarket men not identify with Sir Nigel Gresley's creations — after all, he was an Edinburgh man, like them!

It was Haymarket crews who set the world record for non-stop running of a steam-powered passenger train when, on no fewer than 17 occasions in 1948, they drove the diverted 'Flying Scotsman' via Galashiels non-stop on a run totalling 408 miles. After the arrival of the Class 55 'Deltics' in 1961, the depot staff extended their expertise into this newer field of traction for some 20 years, before IC125s took over the running of the major expresses.

The present depot has a new office building at its east end, with sidings for DMU stock stretching in the direction of Haymarket station. In 1985 it had 25 DMU sets allocated (already averaging more than a quarter of a century old!), and some 74 locomotives, divided into 13 Class 08, 12 Class 20, 33 Class 26 and 16 Class 47/7, at the end of 1986. All Class 47/7s were transferred to Glasgow Eastfield in the following year, and the site is now a Sprinter depot. (See detailed allocation at the end of this book.)

The allocations for both the above sheds seem to confirm the comments of a North Eastern enthusiast, A. B. Allen, writing rather caustically in 1942:

> 'It is difficult to understand how the NB carried on prior to 1923, for take away GN classes A1, D1, J50, K2, K3 and N2, NE C7, J24, and J72, GC D11 and O4, GE F7, J66, and J69, and LNE types A3, A4, D49, J38, J39, K4, P2, V1 and V2, all of which are to be seen in the NB area, and all that remains are dozens of 4-4-0s and 0-6-0s, helped along by a handful of 4-4-2Ts and 0-6-2Ts, helped along by that weird creation the Y9.'

At least Mr Allen has left locomotive historians with an interesting record of contemporary Scottish locomotive denizens, even if he shows considerable ignorance of the financial hamstringing of the NBR at the end of World War 1, in which the company had

loaned locomotives for service abroad and on other lines, such as the Highland. The war was followed by difficulties over suitable government compensation, and the NBR locomotive funds were starved as a result. In any event, it would have been surprising if the LNER, with their world-renowned CME, had not introduced at least *some* new locomotives into the Edinburgh area in the 19 years after Grouping!

Dalry Road

Dalry Road was perhaps the poor relation of the city's main sheds, lacking the allocation of a large stud of high-powered locomotives as at Haymarket less than a mile away, or the multitude of varied duties undertaken by St Margaret's. This former Caledonian shed operated the services run in and out of Princes Street, to Carstairs and Carlisle, Glasgow (Central), Perth via Larbert, and the local branches to Balerno, Barnton, and Leith, as well as freight in and out of the docks at Leith and Granton. Former 'Caley' 4-4-0s and 'Jumbos' 0-6-0s were to be seen here well into the 1960s, and LMS-designed 2-6-4Ts often undertook the running of major expresses as far as Carstairs.

By the end of the last century, when Haymarket had assumed the mantle of Edinburgh's most prestigious engine depot, and St Margaret's was already too crowded for its site, Dalry Road comprised three separate sheds, one of three roads, two each of two, and a turntable near the Dundee Street corner. This last feature was removed around the middle of the 1890s — when a new turntable was installed near the terminus itself — and its former site became the haunt of the shed's 'dead' stock — Pickersgill 4-4-0 No 54478 seemed to be there almost permanently in the last years of 64C. One can only imagine the difficulties in running an MPD without its own turntable!

Towards the end of its life the shed was a four-road dead-end building situated within the triangle formed by the junction of the line to Carstairs (running south of the depot) and the lines to Leith and Haymarket West Junction (running north of the depot, past the island platform station of Dalry Road). There was a manually-operated coaling bank similar to those at St Margaret's and Seafield. Its locomotive allocation, listed at the end of this book, shows nothing more powerful on the passenger side than 'Black Fives', or a solitary 'Crab'

Right:
Standard Class 4MT 2-6-4T No 80027 passes Dalry Road on a local service in April 1955. On the left are withdrawn Compounds Nos 41147/8. Today the route of the former railway lines is followed by Edinburgh's West Approach Road.
G. M. Staddon/N. E. Stead collection

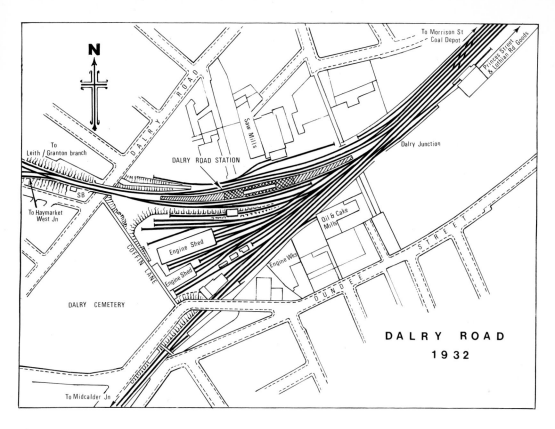

Above:
Dalry Road depot, 1932.

Left:

Dalry Road shed seen from the rear on a summer evening in June 1935. Examples of former CR motive-power visible are, from left to right, '3F' 0-6-0 No 17645, '3F' 0-6-0T No 16228, and '2P' 0-4-4Ts Nos 15156 and 15205. *W. E. Boyd collection*

Bottom left:

Basking in the evening sunshine in August 1926, LMS 4-4-0 No 14345 is photographed from the Dalry Road island platform being coaled at the depot 'next door'. This engine was previously Caledonian 'Dunalastair III' No 896, one of two originally allocated to Edinburgh when outshopped at the turn of the century. Sister engine No 899 ran the 100.5 miles from Carlisle in 97min net during the Race of 1901 and it is quite likely that No 896 was similarly involved on other days in that year. *W. E. Boyd collection*

Below:

Thirty-one years later, 'Jubilee' class 4-6-0 No 45663 *Jervis* is coaled at Dalry Road, alongside Caledonian 0-4-4T No 55165. The 'Jubilee' would have worked the 11.25 Birmingham-Edinburgh.
G. M. Staddon/N. E. Stead collection

2-6-0 for freight work. This underlines the branch nature of the former Caledonian presence in the city — and it was a withering branch, despite the excellent location of Princes Street station.

No trace of this Dalry Road depot now remains, following closure in October 1965, the former Caledonian approach to Princes Street having been taken over by the West Approach Road, and the Dalry Road shed site obliterated. There is equally little left to commemorate Dalry Road shed in railway literature; it had no Charles Meacher or Norman McKillop to record its stories, and seems to have been visited by railway enthusiasts comparatively rarely.

More's the pity! No depot whose locomotives and men could run from Carlisle to Edinburgh in around 97min, including the climb to Beattock and Cobbinshaw summits, as 'Dunalastair III' No 899 did in 1901, deserves such oblivion.

Seafield

Seafield was an unusual depot, having been built by the Caledonian and taken over by the North British during World War 1. The former company never introduced passenger workings on its Trinity-Seafield line and their reduced engine requirements in the area made it convenient for the NBR to acquire the use of the depot when building the Lothian New Lines to bring Lothian coals to Leith. The shed thus sheltered freight locomotives only, nearly all of them former NBR 0-6-0s, from the salt air of the Firth of Forth only a few yards away. There was an open-ended running shed, a turntable, coaling-bank, and not much else! Locomotives reached the rest of the system by crossing Seafield Road on the overbridge and running to Meadows Junction.

In 1945 the shed had 17 engines allocated, with 28 crews divided into two 'links'. The bigger of these, comprising 24 crews was known as the 'coal train link', indicating the depot's staple function. This former sub-shed of St Margaret's no longer exists, and even the sea has been moved! A new sewage treatment plant has been built on reclaimed land to the east of the former breakwater where Seafield shed once sheltered its fleet of 'J35s', 'J36s', 'J37s' and 'J38s'.

Below:
No 64608, one of a sizeable allocation of Class J37 0-6-0s at St Margaret's, at Seafield in August 1955. The Caledonian 'pug' on the left was used for shunting in Leith Docks. *G. M. Staddon/N. E. Stead collection*

Craigentinny CSMD

Craigentinny, between 2½ and 3 miles east of Waverley, has been the main carriage-siding area for Edinburgh for so long (since immediately before World War 1) that it is difficult to realise that it has now taken over Haymarket's role as the motive-power centre for the 'Enginemen Elite', relegating Haymarket to the maids-of-all-work status which St Margaret's once held. For, since 1978, Craigentinny CSMD, as it is now known to railwaymen, has been the servicing centre for Edinburgh's IC125s, with five sets being allocated here, as well as 127 passenger coaches. These include vehicles for the Edinburgh-Glasgow push-pull, Edinburgh-Aberdeen, and Edinburgh-WCML locomotive-hauled services. With the spread of electrification to Edinburgh, it has become the home of Class 91 locomotives, DVTs and Mk 4 coaches.

Two hundred vehicles are received and despatched from here daily, or to be more exact, nightly, when the depot is busiest, with 140 examinations being carried out every 24hr. To utilise the HSTs to their fullest, Craigentinny rostered its own units on London-bound services before 13.00, while servicing visiting sets overnight and then allocating them to north and westbound services out of Waverley in the mornings, scheduling these to return south after 13.00.

Situated on the down side of the ECML, the depot

Above:
Class J37 0-6-0 No 64624 pulls out of Craigentinny with empty coaching stock for Waverley in June 1958.
G. M. Staddon/N. E. Stead collection

has a two-road fuelling-point, a bodyside washing plant, and single-road inspection shed with an 840ft-long centre pit. This is in addition to the two-road maintenance shed with both side and centre pits, all overlooked by a 25-ton overhead crane with a 100ft travel span. South of this is the cleaning shed, with four roads under cover and three outside. Near this area is what is tactfully referred to as the 'controlled emission toilet apron', whose precise function can probably be imagined, and there are appropriate stores buildings at the eastern (Portobello) end. Overspill sidings stretch as far as Portobello East Junction, reaching fully a mile from the turnout from Craigentinny to ECML, along the former alignment of the main line (now relaid to ease the infamous Portobello curve so sensationally traversed by NER No 1621 in 1895 at 66½mph above regulation speed!).

Despite its importance, Craigentinny no longer has the same air of bustling activity which was its main characteristic up to 20 years ago. No longer do steam locomotives — 'V1s', 'V3s' or perhaps named 4-4-0s displaced from main line duties — move empty coaching stock in and out of the sidings, often

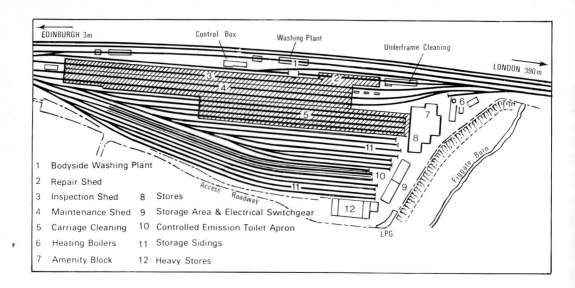

1 Bodyside Washing Plant
2 Repair Shed
3 Inspection Shed   8 Stores
4 Maintenance Shed   9 Storage Area & Electrical Switchgear
5 Carriage Cleaning   10 Controlled Emission Toilet Apron
6 Heating Boilers   11 Storage Sidings
7 Amenity Block   12 Heavy Stores

at front and rear of express rakes bound for the Waverley where a larger engine would then head the train. Modern diesel locomotives are expected to head their own empties! Not only that, but with the loop lines no longer running parallel to the ECML on the up side opposite Craigentinny, local enthusiasts and to a much lesser degree, residents, are no longer able to savour the sight of one of these loops hosting a regular Sunday 'overspill' of up to 20 0-6-0s which St Margaret's was unable to accommodate in its restricted site when no goods train rolled on Sundays.

Craigentinny, which has given its name to IC125 power unit No 43100, no longer sports its 'goal-posts'. Half-way down the yard, there was, even until comparatively recently, a wooden all-over profile loading gauge specifically designed to test clearances on the first corridor tenders to be used by steam locomotives on non-stop workings to and from King's Cross. The modern successors to Gresley's Pacifics have no such clearance problems.

Top left:
Craigentinny CSMD 1987.

Left:
With an ECML express, 'A1' Pacific No 60160 *Auld Reekie* passes Craigentinny signalbox in August 1958.
G. M. Staddon/N. E. Stead collection

Above:
Viewed from one of the lighting pylons, Craigentinny CSMD stretches eastwards, with the Portobello Freightliner gantry in the background and Jewel and Esk Valley College on the horizon. Locomotive-hauled stock is prominent in this photograph which shows, from left to right respectively, the single-line Inspection Shed, double-track Maintenance Shed, and further away the quadruple-track and cleaning building.
ScotRail

Overleaf:
The Maintenance Shed interior Craigentinny, complete with side and centre inspection pits. *ScotRail*

11
Edinburgh's Smaller Termini

From east to west, and excluding Leith, there were branch line termini at Musselburgh, Granton, Barnton, Corstorphine, and Balerno. All are now closed to passengers. Strictly speaking Balerno was not a branch terminus, being situated on a loop line off the Caledonian main line between Slateford and Ravelrig Junction.

Similarly, **Musselburgh** should not really be considered in this book, as 'the Honest Toun' has always been staunchly independent of the capital. Its small fishing harbour of Fisherrow was originally reached by a branch from the Edinburgh & Dalkeith. Part of this was incorporated into the NBR's later double-track Musselburgh branch from the East Coast main line at New Hailes Junction in 1847, but the Fisherrow line still crossed the A1 by level-crossing well into the 1950s. Sidings existed between the sands and road in the Joppa direction, an area now grassed over.

The main Musselburgh branch terminus comprised a single non-island platform, partly covered by a wooden roof spanning two tracks. There was an engine shed here at one time and behind the platform a siding giving access to the neighbouring wireworks for which the town has always been famous. DMUs were introduced on the line from 1958, but closure followed only six years later, the station site being too far from the town-centre.

Musselburgh's terminus has now been obliterated by recent road developments in the area.

A new station was recently opened on the ECML at Monktonhall, to the south of Musselburgh, served by North Berwick trains. Although not enjoying the central location of the former NBR terminus, its isolation has been lessened by the growth of Musselburgh southwards.

As previously mentioned, **Granton** owed its branch line from Waverley (originally Canal Street) to its ferry connections to Burntisland in Fife. This formed the original Edinburgh-Aberdeen 'main line' before the opening of the Forth Bridge and as a result the world's first train ferry, the *Leviathan*, started operating from here in the late 1840s.

There was a station at Trinity nearby, complete with a ticket-window exclusively for the use of fishwives taking their fresh wares to sell on the city's doorsteps, and a wind-vane in the form of a clock-face. This instrument, still extant on the station building (now a private residence), advised passengers what passage to expect when alighting

Below:
North British 'J88' 0-6-0T No 68340 sits just off the roadway at Granton Square in August 1955, with Granton Pier stretching into the left distance.
G. M. Staddon/N. E. Stead collection

at Trinity station for a ferry passage from the Old Chain Pier then a few yards away. The pier's ferry role was almost immediately taken over by the new port of Granton built by the Duke of Buccleuch and the Chain Pier itself has long since been destroyed by storm. Unlike Trinity, no station artifacts remain in the Granton area, now bustling with oil-related business and cash and carry warehouses.

With the opening of the Forth Bridge in 1890, a passenger service continued to Granton until 1925, before succumbing to tram competition. Its closure was an administrative shambles, the LNER making no attempt to anticipate public reaction to their closure proposals. Only 10 days notice of withdrawal was given, but a protest petition of 300 signatures was collected in a third of that time. The company had a reasonable case for wishing to withdraw services, and was able to refute one complainant's point about the irony of a rail company operating a ferry with no rail passenger connection by pointing out that the ferry was busiest on Sundays when the branch's passenger trains did not operate.

Nevertheless, a local solicitor gave the LNER a fright by taking up the matter with his MP, Capt Wedgwood Benn, father to the well-known present-day politician. The Ministry of Transport now asked the company to justify closure all over again, and the LNER's officers must have wished they had at least held a public meeting to air their reasons for closure. All this was before the foundation of the Transport Users' Consultative Committees in 1947, and the Granton case amply underlines the necessity of their existence when the vast postwar closure programme

loomed. Suffice to say that after considerable manoeuvring behind the scenes the LNER's management in Scotland was able to convince the Ministry, and the local lawyer, of their case.

Granton was until 1987 Britain's last major centre for gas-producing (as opposed to processing North

Below:
Granton Gas Works station pictured in 1934. This was a private terminus for gasworks employees travelling to and from Princes Street by their own services, powered by the Caledonian and later the LMS, until 1942. These travelled to and from the west side of Granton by a branch off the Leith branch at the 'other' Crewe junction, although in fact Granton was opened to freight before Leith. This scene is unrecognisable now. North British traffic could have reached the eastern side of the complex by the steeply-graded line shown on the right, travelling through an area that was industrialised after this picture was taken. Two of the Works' Barclay tanks can be seen in the picture; the complex also had a 2ft gauge system. *Real Photos*

Top right:
Barnton station building seen from the road in 1950, shortly before closure. This survived in use for commercial premises until almost the time of writing. *Real Photos*

Right:
Looking perfect for a modelling project, Barnton station is seen in LMS days around 1934. One academic study of Barnton has shown that the suburb's growth coincided with the closing of the station in 1951, suggesting that the railway made little impact here. *Real Photos*

Sea gas), its huge towers forming the capital's most prominent artificial landmarks when viewed from the sea. This complex had no fewer than three rail approaches, one of them lasting until 1986. An extension of the NBR branch approached the works up a steep gradient from the east, and this was the scene of a terrifying runaway, graphically described by Charles Meacher in his book *LNER Footplate Memories*. A related set of sidings entered through the portals of the former Caroline Park estate from a branch running beside the sea westwards from the harbour, and the works themselves were also served by the Caledonian from the Crewe Toll area. The western side of the complex even had its own passenger station with workmen's services to Princes Street as late as 1942, and the building is

still standing at the time of writing. Indeed as late as April 1987, the complex still had tracks *in situ* despite being cut off from the BR system!

Barnton is nowadays a pleasant suburb which can claim to be as near a 'stockbroker belt' as any part of Edinburgh is likely to be. Ironically, its development really got under way after World War 2, and one geographer studying the city's transport scene has commented that the suburb's increase in size coincided with the closure of its branch railway!

This was a delightful line built by the Caledonian Railway from Princes Street. The branch ran from the company's Granton and Leith line just north of Craigleith station, through Davidson's Mains to terminate in what appears to have been a highly

Above:
Corstorphine station building, seen from the roadside on a wet July day in 1954. The tracks were at right angles to the main building, facing eastwards in the direction of Waverley, which could be reached in only 11min. *Real Photos*

Left:
Corstorphine terminus in 1924, with former NER Class S 4-6-0 No 2007 waiting to leave with the 13.17 ECS to Waverley, forming the 13.30 thence to Berwick-on-Tweed. Main line engines were not uncommon at Corstorphine on such duties, even after the introduction of DMUs on services from here to North Berwick from the end of the 1950s. *W. E. Boyd collection*

Below:
The Corstorphine branch left the main lines west from Waverley, at Balgreen Halt, seen here in 1967 with a Waverley-bound Cravens DMU. *N. E. Stead collection*

Top:
A Gloucester DMU at Pinkhill station in 1967, bound for Corstorphine. Pinkhill served nearby Edinburgh Zoo.
N. E. Stead collection

Above:
Corstorphine terminus in July 1959 with Ivatt '2MT' 2-6-0 No 46462, having arrived with the 17.18 from Waverley. This utilised the stock from the 17.03 arrival from Inverness, which was then stabled overnight at Corstorphine. *G. M. Staddon/N. E. Stead collection*

attractive little terminus, then called Cramond Brig, just north of the present Barnton Roundabout. The village of Davidson's Mains had a station on the line, with a goods station at a lower level, on a site now occupied by a supermarket. After the LMS took over the line in 1923 it built a halt in the House o' Hill vicinity. The line closed in 1951 but the Barnton terminal building stood until recently, in use for commecial purposes, not far from the roar of traffic on its way to and from the Forth Road Bridge. Small wonder that the branch failed to prosper, given that it could only connect residents, who are among the city's most affluent and include a huge proportion of motorists, with the city's west end easily reached by road.

Proceeding westwards, or in an anti-clockwise direction in this survey of Edinburgh's termini, brings us to **Corstorphine**. This was not the first station of the name, as Saughton station, built at what later became the junction of the Glasgow and Forth Bridge routes out of Waverley originally held this name, despite being some distance from the village of Corstorphine.

In contrast the Corstorphine terminus opened in 1902 was situated in the heart of the village, a short distance from the main Glasgow road. The terminus had two platforms with the station buildings behind the buffer stops. Destinations offered included East Coast centres beyond Waverley, with a daily Edinburgh to Berwick-on-Tweed service beginning its southward journey from here after World War 1, although the Corstorphine-Waverley journey was often run as ECS. North Berwick was another destination, a DMU service connecting the two branch termini from 1958. If, at that time, a railway enthusiast had been asked which of them was to close within 10 years, would he have settled on the terminus in a dormitory suburb a few miles from the centre of the city, with chronic traffic jams on the nearby main-road, or the (admittedly delightful) holiday resort at the end of a remote branch some 20 miles out from the capital?

Undeniably, the Corstorphine line's main feature was its ability to speed passengers in and out of Waverley in a few minutes, a feat which the modern traveller must now view with envy. Compare even the wartime timetable which allowed steam tank locomotives 11min to travel from here to Waverley, in contrast to the 22min now optimistically scheduled for the LRT bus. It seems inexplicable that the line should have closed at the end of 1967 when the neighbouring trunk road westwards was shortly destined to channel virtually all the city's traffic to the M8 and M9 motorways into its two lanes in Corstorphine's main street.

Also lost to BR's traffic receipts ledger is excursion traffic to and from Edinburgh Zoo, Scotland's biggest and most impressive park of its kind. This was served on the branch by the two-platformed Pinkhill station within earshot of the roars of the Californian sealions. Taken with the commuter traffic in and out of Corstorphine, the branch's closure still remains, to this author at least, one of the most inexplicable BR has ever carried out.

Long departed now from the transport map is the **Balerno** branch, one of the services furnished by the Caledonian from Princes Street. As already indicated, Balerno was situated on a through line six miles long, leaving the Princes Street-Carstairs main line just west of Slateford station, immediately crossing the Union Canal, and then following the charming valley of the Water of Leith, crossing the river five times. With intermediate stations at Colinton, Juniper Green, and Currie, services were inaugurated to Balerno from 1874. Balerno was regarded as the line's terminus, although the line proceeded further west to rejoin the Carstairs line at Ravelrig Junction.

It is doubtful if the Caledonian envisaged this as a through alternative route to its main line, even for emergency diversionary purposes, as the line's curves were so sharp as to render necessary the use of short-wheelbase rolling stock whenever possible. Indeed, four-wheel passenger stock was still being built for the services after World War 1. These were delivered by R. Y. Pickering & Co of Wishaw in 1922, an eight-coach set of these vehicles weighing all of 111 tons tare, replete with velvet pile rugs in first class! In 1935 there were 20 passenger trains each way daily on the line, with no fewer than nine Sunday services for day-trippers visiting the nearby Pentland Hills.

The Balerno line must have been one of the city's most delightful, as a walk along its course, by virtue of a modern walkway, will show. Leaving the canal towpath near Kingsknowe it is possible to pass the site of the former Hailes platform, built for Kingsknowe's golfers in 1927, and plunge into Colinton Dell, with the river out of sight to the left. Colinton station site is reached after a stroll through a curved tunnel, opening immediately on to a platform on the right-hand side.

From this point on, there is vestigal evidence of a surprising amount of industry in this sylvan environment — papermills, quarries, a tannery, and a naticnally famous salt-making concern in days

Top right:
Gresley Class V3 2-6-2T No 67615 pulls out of Pinkhill on the last stage of its journey to Corstorphine in January 1960. *G. M. Staddon/N. E. Stead collection*

Right:
Juniper Green, a delightful wayside halt on the Balerno branch, photographed in 1934. This was some nine years before closure to passengers. *Real Photos*

Above:

'Balerno pug' 0-4-4T No 15151 stands at the Dalry Road coaling stage around 1930. Note that the LMS have replaced the original Caledonian works plate above the leading driving wheel. *Real Photos*

gone by. So important was goods traffic in the area that it hung on for nearly a quarter of a century after passenger withdrawal. Gone now are the papermills, working to feed the city's printing and publishing industry, and their sites have either been levelled, as at the former Juniper Green station site, or adapted to form small workshop accommodation, as at Kinleith, near Currie.

Balerno's branch closure is as much of a transport tragedy as Corstorphine's. While the latter could have adopted an increasingly useful role in the transport network of the Lothians, one cannot help feeling that the Balerno line, at least in the Colinton area, would have been a picturesque candidate for a preservation project.

Why did Edinburgh's internal rail services fail? Because of Waverley's location, the 'Sub' platforms (20 and 21) making the problem worse. The city's commuters included a high proportion of motorists among their professional classes — by the time

much-needed parking controls had been imposed on the city-centre, the suburban rail services were moribund. Also, the tram service was so good, as indeed is the present bus service, following a temporary decline in standards during the 50s and 60s.

In contrast, ScotRail has shown admirable initiative in reopening the **Bathgate** branch, from 24 March 1986. This is the stub of the former through line between Waverley and Glasgow (Queen Street Low Level), leaving the main former NBR line between Waverley and Queen Street at Newbridge, some nine miles west of the city. Glasgow was reached through Bathgate (Lower and Upper) stations and Airdrie on a line closed to passenger traffic in 1956.

Thirty years later may have seemed an inappropriate time to reintroduce the service. The British Leyland plant was running down towards closure with heavy redundancies when a £1.5 million scheme was set in motion to put Bathgate back on the railway map. Co-operating with BR were the Scottish Development Agency (for the Government), Lothian Regional Council, West Lothian District Council, Livingston Development Corporation, aided by European funding. The nearby new town of

Livingston thus gained a new station (one of two on the branch, the other being at Uphall), and this supplemented its new halt serving the south of Livingston on the Edinburgh-Glasgow line via Shotts.

With much of the initiative for the Bathgate line coming from the Scottish Office, cynics have suggested that the Government made this reopening possible to distract from Bathgate's increasing isolation from the industrial scene. In any event, it was illogical to have a 75,000 catchment area lacking a railway, so residents of Bathgate and Livingston can now commute into Haymarket within 29min and Waverley within 33.

At the end of the service's first year ScotRail was gratified to discover that half-a-million tickets had been sold for the Bathgate Link, almost two-thirds up on estimate — and despite the disappointing continued use of 1950s DMU stock. Obviously subscribing to the old military adage of 'always reinforce success', ScotRail and Provincial sector managers designated the Bathgate line to be the first in Scotland to be operated by Class 150 'Sprinters'.

Meanwhile, other areas west of the city recently placed on the rail map are Wester Hailes and Curriehill. The former, as already mentioned, is a huge council housing-area, mainly comprising former Leith residents. It had never been well-served by public facilities, and its present station is long overdue. In contrast, Curriehill, slightly to the west, is seen as a potential 'park (or kiss) and ride' facility.

Both stations are on the former Caledonian main line and should bring considerable revenue benefits to the Waverley-West Calder and Glasgow (Central) services.

Below:
The 14.06 Edinburgh-Bathgate train nears its destination in June 1988 formed of Class 150/2 'Sprinter' No 150283. The line is actually single and the nearside track was rusted and out of use. *Brian Morrison*

12
The 'Sub' and Other Points South

From time to time the local Edinburgh newspaper, the *Evening News*, carries a plea — or a report of the occasional consultant's plan — for the reopening to passengers of the Southside suburban circle, or 'the Sub' as it is usually known.

Indeed in 1986, Edinburgh District Council went so far as to commission the local Napier College's Transport Research Group to investigate the possibility of such a revival, and the result was a blueprint for the reopening of five, and setting up of three more, stations to carry 1.68 million passengers annually at the remarkably low estimated cost (excluding rolling stock) of £1.25 million. Unfortunately, ScotRail appeared lukewarm to the idea from the start, and such a reopening seems unlikely at the time of writing, particularly since the punitive imposition of a Government ruling requiring an 8% return on capital investment.

Such is the public interest in the line that every time an excursion train is sent round the 'Sub' it is invariably packed — at Christmas 1986 no fewer than 12 specials had to be run to take passengers from Waverley to right back where they had started from, although admittedly the haulage power of preserved steam locomotives such as 0-6-0 *Maude* was a contributing attraction (to say nothing of Santa Claus, with presents for younger travellers). On the other hand, only a few months previously a nondescript Class 26 had hauled eight crowded coaches full of non-railway enthusiast excursionists round the circle. So why should BR be reluctant to reopen the line, particularly if local authority support seems likely to be available?

The author lives so close to this line that his word processor shakes with the passing of every train. And there are plenty of these, which may increase

Left:
Maude on the 'Sub'. Preserved lovingly by the SRPS, Class 'C' 0-6-0 (LNER 'J36') No 673 enjoys a pre-Christmas outing on a 'Santa Special'. She is seen climbing towards Morningside Road from the east on 15 December 1985. *M. Macdonald*

Above:
Although laid out as recently as the early 1960s, Millerhill Down yard has already had its tracks lifted, and the doubts voiced about its siting by the late Gerard Fiennes in the Ian Allan book *I Tried to Run a Railway* appear well founded. This June 1980 picture shows No 26004 heading a trip working northwards to South Leith. *M. Macdonald*

ScotRail's reluctance to reintroduce passenger services. For this constitutes one of the busiest freight-only lines in the Scottish network, although the closure of the Portobello Freightliner depot has caused a slight decline in its traffic. A glance at the map will show why this line is so important at the present time.

From the east the 'Sub' takes traffic from Millerhill yard at Niddrie West Junction, where until recently a single-line also joined from the ECML at Monktonhall Junction. This, somewhat strangely, has been lifted, despite its obvious advantage of offering a direct diversionary route for northbound traffic from the ECML without the necessity of it going round at Millerhill, as will now be the case. (Freight trains between the ECML and the 'Sub'

usually have their engines changed at Millerhill or their locomotives run round the train here, although a through connection by way of the yard sidings is physically possible.)

Also at Niddrie West, a single line trails in from Portobello East and Niddrie North Junctions — this would constitute the eastern arm of the circle if a suburban service was reintroduced round from Waverley. Niddrie West also enjoyed, until 1967, a direct connection from South Leith via the Lothian lines. This was highly appropriate, given that this area was, in earlier years, effectively the crucial centre of the old Edinburgh & Dalkeith Railway, and until recently an embankment was still visible pointing northwestwards from the junction through Portobello to South Leith — the archaeological remains of the old E&D branch.

No description of this rail complex at Niddrie can be made without mentioning the former NCB rail network which served the Newcraighall and Woolmet pits, and which exchanged traffic with BR on the south side of Niddrie West Junction. Steam 'pugs' shunted wagons about here until 1972, frequently creating an air of Wild West railroading, with the sight of two or more tank engines pushing and pulling their load of empties over the Newcraighall Road and then up the ramshackle track, like tugs buffeting through rough weather, southwards to Woolmet colliery. Yet all this was taking place within the city boundary and within four miles of Waverley!

Above:
Class 25 No 25064 heads a train of gas pipes from South Leith across Portobello East Junction on to the turnoff leading (at one time) to the Waverley Route or the Suburban Circle. The '25' will take the latter line before heading northwards to Montrose after regaining the London-Aberdeen line at Haymarket West Junction on the other side of the city, thus avoiding reversing. An '08' shunter can just be seen in the background, between the abutments of the former Lothian lines viaduct (on the South Leith-Niddrie North single-line), shunting at what used to be the turnout from Joppa yard on to the ECML. *M. Macdonald*

Below:
No passenger train has been timetabled to run on the Glencorse branch since 1933, but the line was kept busy with MGR traffic to and from Bilston Glen, some four miles from Millerhill, where the branch joins the former Waverley Route. In this September 1977 view east of Gilmerton No 26006, geared for slow-speed running over the hoppers at Cockenzie, heads a MGR train for that power station. *M. Macdonald*

Moving westwards, the 'Sub' passed through Niddrie yards, an important marshalling point for locally-produced coal, but also for Anglo-Scottish freight arrivals from both the Carlisle and Newcastle directions. Indeed, not so many years back, the famous mid-afternoon freight departure from London's King's Cross Depot, the '266 Down', terminated here.

This was before the opening of Millerhill yard, a couple of miles to the southeast, and situated on a green-field site that was not above criticism. In his bitter-sweet book of practical railway memories *I Tried to Run a Railway*, the late Gerard Fiennes criticises the location of the Millerhill yard, preferring a site nearer Glasgow, Scotland's major industrial base. Today's vista of the empty and overgrown sidings at Millerhill, closed entirely on the down side, would certainly suggest he was right. The trend away from single wagon to multiple loads at a time of freight being lost to road has of course rendered obsolete the huge capacity of these yards, and the closure of the Waverley Route (surely likely to the planners in the 1950s), has made Millerhill an even bigger white elephant than before. Nowadays, the complex is used as a PW materials site, and the diesel depot is used for servicing only.

The most important new facility in the area is the Electrification Fixed Equipment Construction Depot opened on 13 April, 1987. This is a £1.25 million site immediately to the south of Millerhill yard. It runs 1km south from the former site of Millerhill station, where a spur from Monktonhall Junction arrives from the ECML in the northeastern direction and meets the Bilston branch from the southwestern.

Railway historians will not need to be told that the depot is in fact nothing more than a mini-resurrection of part of the old, much-lamented, Waverley Route! Now its function is to house stockpiles of steel masts, administration cabins (moved from Barassie on the now-completed Ayrline project) for 170 staff, with a concrete batching plant dominating the new area. It was all plain sailing for the construction contractors — once they managed to discover the exact whereabouts of a forgotten mineshaft two centuries old. Grout had to be pumped into the shaft, which was no less than 265ft deep and 10ft wide. Now the Waverley Route is making a major contribution to the modernisation of another, more fortunate, main line.

So back to the 'Sub', which now takes us to the north of the huge council housing estate of Craigmillar, served until 1962 by Duddingston & Craigmillar station. Duddingston is a picturesque village now enveloped by suburban estates to the north of the line; the station was badly-situated for both communities. Immediately to the east of the former station was the junction of the St Leonard's branch, leading to Edinburgh's first station. Its single line crossed the main Duddingston Road at Cairntows Crossing, then headed along the southern shore of Duddingston Loch bird sanctuary before plunging into the depths (or more accurately heights, given the 1 in 30 rising gradient) of the formerly gaslit tunnel to St Leonard's. From 1912 to 1961 this branch was almost exclusively the responsibility of J88 tank engine No 68338, at one time being sub-shedded at the branch terminus itself.

Both Duddingston and St Leonard's were major brewing centres until comparatively recently, using the area's excellent natural springs, but the next part of the 'Sub's' journey is almost pastoral, the 822ft volcanic pile of Arthur's Seat dominating the view to the north. After passing the huge hypermarket at Cameron Toll — naturally enough, specified as a probable stopping-place in any reintroduction of passenger services — the line skirts Newington Cemetery, recently disfigured by giant hogweed. The former Newington station was, unusually, an island platform, well-placed for the local community with a tram terminus next to the station building on the A7.

A westbound freight is now starting to notice an adverse incline, continuing past the former site of Blackford Hill station, with the Royal Observatory brooding above on the flank of the hill of that name. The climb continues at around 1 in 85 almost until Morningside Road station. This was a substantial two-platform stopping-place, whose station building was very conveniently situated at a major crossroads. Indeed, so optimistically was the railway welcomed to Morningside that a large building suitable for hotel accommodation was erected a few yards away on the other side of the crossroads. This has always been a private residence since opening, but its very appearance suggests a railway's presence, even if the passer-by were unable to hear the roar of diesels grinding up to Morningside from east or west. For this is the summit of the 'Sub', as well as formerly the busiest station.

The reopening of the entire 'Sub' could be too much for ScotRail to contemplate — it would virtually require the construction from scratch of stations at Blackford, Newington, Cameron Toll, and Niddrie/Asda — while recent proposals for a Metro by the ruling Labour group on Lothian Region, and a third-rail 'Speedlink' from their Conservative opposition, have made the whole issue increasingly complex.

From Morningside, continuing our imaginary tour of the line, the westbound train is travelling downhill, gradually at first, but then quite steeply through Craiglockhart station, set deep in a brick cutting. The station here was built three years later than the others, in 1887, and was not perhaps ideally situated. Immediately after the station, the line dives under Colinton Road and the Union Canal, railway-owned for most of its working life, to come

Above:

With Arthur's Seat brooding in the right background, Reid 'Intermediate' 4-4-0 No 9892 stands at Duddingston & Craigmillar station on the (Inner) Suburban Circle on 25 August 1938. Originally allocated to the old NBR shed at Berwick-on-Tweed, this locomotive (classified 'D32' by the LNER) worked from St Margaret's on passenger trains for most of her existence, which ended in 1948. *W. E. Boyd collection*

Below:

A Gloucester DMU at Duddingston on a Musselburgh service in March 1962 – complete with tail lamp. It has arrived from Waverley and will reverse and enter the right-hand platform for the journey to Musselburgh via Waverley. *G. M. Staddon/N. E. Stead collection*

Top:
Class J37 0-6-0 No 64537 heads an oil train through the former Newington station in May 1964.
G. M. Staddon/N. E. Stead collection

Above:
In April 1964 Gresley Class A3 Pacific No 60100 *Spearmint* heads a freight from Millerhill to Aberdeen past the Blackford Hill signalbox.
G. M. Staddon/N. E. Stead collection

upon a junction constructed in 1960 connecting the former NBR 'Sub' with the former Caledonian main line immediately to the east of Slateford station. Obviously, this now enables the through movement of freight from the Carstairs line or the Glasgow direction towards Millerhill or the East Coast route and vice versa. Track engineers have a depot immediately to the east of Slateford station.

Falling grades now bring our imaginary train to the few remains of Gorgie East station, past a formerly notable network of lines (closed December 1967) penetrating some three-quarters of a mile to Gorgie cattle-market on the south western side. The 'Sub' is now nearing its conclusion, splitting at Gorgie Junction to head westwards to Haymarket West Junction, thus giving access to the former NBR main lines to Glasgow and Aberdeen, or eastwards at Haymarket Central Junction, and thence back to Waverley.

Above:
Blackford Hill station in June 1958, with Ivatt '2MT' No 46461 on the 13.41 inner circle train. In the early 1950s the station entrance was on the first floor, above the door marked 'Private', and there was a footbridge across to the outer circle platforms.
G. M. Staddon/N. E. Stead collection

Top right:
A typical Edinburgh suburban train of the 1950s: 'V1' 2-6-2T No 67666 glides into Morningside Road station in May 1958 with the 13.41 inner circle train from Waverley. *G. M. Staddon/N. E. Stead collection*

Right:
Class J36 No 65224 *Mons* at Morningside Road in April 1956. *G. M. Staddon/N. E. Stead collection*

Left:
'Glen' class 4-4-0 No 62487 *Glen Arklet* heads an inner circle train into Craiglockhart station in July 1955. The wooden footbridge above the train was replaced the next day; the trams on the Colinton route lasted only until October the same year.
G. M. Staddon/N. E. Stead collection

Bottom left:
With steam escaping from every pore, 'V1' 2-6-2T No 67659 pulls out of Gorgie East station in April 1958.
G. M. Staddon/N. E. Stead collection

Below:
Preserved A4 Pacific No 60009 *Union of South Africa* (now *Osprey*) heads eastwards at Lochend Junction on the Abbeyhill-Piershill loop, once part of the Suburban Outer Circle, with a SRPS special on 27 April 1985. Above the first and second coaches can be seen the trackbed of the former spur to Leith Central, enabling trains from that station to reach Waverley after a circuit of the Suburban Circle through Portobello. Not visible above the fifth coach is the spur going down to cross beneath the former Waverley-Leith Central line to connect up with the North Leith/Granton branch at Easter Road.
M. Macdonald

Promoted nominally as a private venture, the Edinburgh, Suburban & Southside Junction Railway, was in fact operated by the North British from the outset in 1884. Although originally surveyed by Sir Thomas Bouch (of Tay Bridge infamy), his plans for the line were not used, compensation being paid to his estate. The only major differences in Bouch's planned course for the line, compared with what was finally built, were the lack of any connection with the St Leonard's branch, and a Y-shaped junction at the east end of the Circle, at Portobello, on the site of the present-day municipal golf course.

Besides tapping the considerable traffic potential of the southern city suburbs, the 'Sub' has always offered the facility of a diversionary route away from Waverley. It is not known if any regular Anglo-Scottish express passenger services were scheduled to take this route to avoid Waverley, although at the time of the line's opening there was considerable speculation in the railway press that this was both likely and desirable, in view of Waverley's chaotic conditions.

Of course, as soon as the NBR embarked on its costly rebuilding of Waverley station in the 1890s it

'would be likely to use the new station to the utmost, and especially constructed a through suburban island platform (later numbered Nos 20 and 21) on the south side of the Waverley for circular services. From October 1903 many of these began or finished their journeys at Leith Central, after completing one circuit. After closure of Leith Central in 1952, 'Sub' trains were operated as a true circle service, including the two stations on the Abbeyhill-Piershill loop, with 'Outer Circle' trains heading eastwards from Waverley, and 'Inner Circle' taking the opposite direction.

Twenty-five years after its opening, an English visitor commented on the surprising number of tender-engines operating passenger trains on the Suburban circle. Possibly, the NBR's Drummond tanks found the climb to Morningside too arduous — although it must be said that these were the same engines operating the Leith Central locals, with all

the hill-climbing that entailed, some 16 of these trains being programmed to traverse the 'Sub' from Leith in each direction every day. W. P. Reid, that most underrated of locomotive designers, certainly eased the problem with his introduction of Class M and L 4-4-2Ts (LNER 'C15' and 'C16') which held sway on most Edinburgh suburban services until the arrival of Gresley's 'V1' 2-6-2Ts in 1930. These then held a virtual monopoly of services on Edinburgh's south side until the arrival of DMUs in 1958.

Despite the introduction of these Gloucester RC&W units, passenger services on the line lasted only another four years before withdrawal. Wholesale closure to passengers hardly seemed to make sense at the time, or in retrospect. Receipts

Above:
Freight on the 'Sub' – 3 – Class 40 No 40063, for many years a Haymarket engine, brings an Oxwellmains-Aberdeen cement train out of the Craiglockhart tunnel, past the Slateford turnoff, on its way to join the line northwards at Haymarket West Junction. This winter view was taken on 21 March 1980. *M. Macdonald*

from Craiglockhart and Blackford Hill stations were probably poor at any time, but a speeded-up service encompassing Gorgie, Morningside, Newington, Craigmillar (possibly resited farther eastwards), and Portobello, would surely have been worth persevering with, particularly since there was no question of saving money by complete abandonment — indeed, at least one of the station buildings was kept in use for freight and parcel purposes for another six years.

The author's last scheduled trip round the 'Sub' included an apparently endless wait for time at Duddingston and Craigmillar — causing considerable grumbling among the passengers. Closure came in 1962 with no attempt to streamline the timetable in the manner suggested, or to save costs by introducing unstaffed halts. There was no apparent will to save the service at all, but wasn't that very much the order of the day in the early 1960s?

Nowadays the line is heavily used by freight — everything from cement cargoes, chemicals, oil, vehicle trains from the Midlands to and from West Lothian (after reversal at Millerhill), and PW and electrification trains operating out of Millerhill. A new addition to the 'Sub's' traffic is the operation of refuse trains from the site of the former Powderhall station to Kaimes quarry on the Carstairs line,

following the circle route and its spur to the former CR main line at Slateford. This will presumably be the route chosen for nuclear waste materials making their way from the new Torness power station to Sellafield, something the local communities in south Edinburgh will scarcely relish.

Over the last few years the variety of diesel locomotives seen on the line has changed, and to some extent diminished. At the time of writing Class 20s are a rarity, only to be seen working in tandem, while the ever-present 26s (a stalwart servant of Scottish locomotive men) are more often seen on electrification trains than on revenue-earning services. Class 37s and 47s still abound — the latter monopolising the new refuse trains from Powderhall to Kaimes — but 56s are now making an appearance, along with the occasional 60.

The only passenger workings are the occasional excursion (often steam-hauled), or diversionary workings, as when Haymarket south tunnel was closed in 1989, causing Edinburgh-southwest England traffic to be diverted via Portobello and the 'sub'. The circular nature of the route also proves useful for ensuring that rigid coaching rakes leave Waverley in the correct configuration. For example, royal train stock has been seen recently traversing the line.

So passenger vehicles are still frequently seen on the 'Sub'; whether a new passenger *service* will make a Phoenix-like appearance is anyone's guess. Equally possible would be complete abandonment, particularly since the catenary is not scheduled to stretch round the south side of Edinburgh, thus reducing the line's value as a diversionary route.

Bibliography

Acworth, W. M.; *The Railways of Scotland*; 1890.

Clinker's Register of Closed Passenger Stations, 2nd edition 1971.

Cornwell, H. J. C.; *Forty Years of Caledonian Locomotives, 1882-1922.*

Croughton et al; *Private & Untimetabled Railway Stations*; 1982.

Dott, George; *Early Scottish Colliery Wagonways*; 1947.

Dow, George; *The First Railway Across the Border*; 1946.

Edinburgh & Leith Post Office Directories.

Ellis, C. H.; *The North British Railway.*

Hassan, J. A.; 'The Supply of Coal to Edinburgh, 1790-1850'; In *Transport History*, Vol 5, 1972.

Hunter, D. L. G.; *Edinburgh's Transport*; Huddersfield, 1964. *From SMT to Eastern Scottish*; Edinburgh, 1987.

Industrial Railway Society; *Industrial Locomotives of Scotland*; Handbook N, 1976.

Lewis, M. J. T.; *Early Wooden Railways.*

Lizars, W. H.; *Lizars' Guide to the Edinburgh Railways*; 1842.

Lowe, James W.; *British Steam Locomotive Builders*; 1975.

Macdonald, M.; *Scotland's Freight Only Lines*; Pennine, 1985.

McKillop, Norman; *Enginemen Elite.*

Meacher, C.; *LNER Footplate Memories.*

Measom, G.; *The Official Illustrated Guide to the Lancaster & Carlisle, Edinburgh & Glasgow, and Caledonian Railways*; 1859.

Moorfoot Publishing; *The Last Trains* (1); 1979.

Page, P. J.; *The Influence of Public Transport on Edinburgh's Development*; Edinburgh University thesis, 1972.

RCTS; *Locomotives of the London North Eastern Railway.*

RCTS (Scottish branch); *Yesteryear's Railway — Edinburgh.*

Robertson, C. J. A.; *The History of the Scottish Railway System.*

Thomas, J.; *The North British Railway*, Vols 1 & 2. *Regional History of Railways of Great Britain, Vol 6 Scotland: Lowlands and Borders.*

Whishaw, Francis; *Whishaw's Railways of Great Britain and Ireland*; 1840 and 1842 editions.

Below:
'K3' class 2-6-0 No 61854 passes Portobello station in July 1960 on the 12.00 Waverley-Carlisle stopping train. The GNR tender is noteworthy.
G. M. Staddon/N. E: Stead collection

Appendices

1 Edinburgh's Passsenger Stations from 1831

Name	Opened – by	Closed – by	No of p'form edges	Nearest road	Remarks
Abbeyhill	1869 – NB	1964 – BR	2	London Rd (A1)	
Balerno	1874 – CR	1943 – LM	1	Station Loan	
Balgreen Halt	1934 – LN	1967 – BR	2	Balgreen Road	
Barnton	1894 – CR	1951 – BR	2	Whitehouse Road	
Barnton Gate					*See* Davidson's Mains
Blackford Hill	1884 – NB	1962 – BR	2	B'ford Avenue	Closed 1917-9
Bonnington Rd	1847 – EL	1947 – LN	2	Newhaven Road	Closed 1917-9
Canal St	1847 – EL	1868 – NB	2	Waverley Bridge	Named 'Princes St' for a time
Colinton	1874 – CR	1943 – LM	1	Bridge Rd	
Corstorphine	1902 – NB	1967 – BR	2	Station Rd	*See also* Saughton
Craigleith	1879 – CR	1962 – BR	2	Queensferry Road	
Craiglockhart	1887 – NB	1962 – BR	2	Colinton Rd	Closed 1917-9
Cramond Brig					*See* Barnton
Currie	1874 – CR	1943 – LM	2	Station Road, Currie	
Curriehill (1)	1850s – CR	1951 – BR	2	Kiers Hill Rd	
Curriehill (2)	1987 – BR		2		
Dalry Road	1900 – CR	1962 – BR	2	Dalry Rd/Dundee Street	
Davidson's Mains	1894 – CR	1951 – BR	2	Barnton Avenue	
Duddingston & Craigmillar	1884 – NB	1962 – BR	2	Duddingston Rd W	
East Pilton	1934 – LM	1962 – BR	2	Crewe Rd N	
Easter Road	c1895 – NB	1947 – LN	2	Easter Road	Closed 1917-9
Easter Road Park	1950 – BR	1967 – BR	1	Hawkhill Ave	Football halt
Fisherrow	1830s – ED	1847 – NB	1	Musselburgh Rd	
General					*See* Waverley
Gilmerton	1874 – NB	1933 – LN	1	Off A7	Closed 1917-9
Gorgie East	1884 – NB	1962 – BR	2	Slateford Road	
Granton	1846 – EL	1925 – LN	1	Granton Sq	Ferry terminal Closed 1917-9
Granton Gasworks	1902 – CR	1942 – LM	2		Private
Granton Rd	1874 – CR	1962 – BR	2	Granton Road	
Hailes	1927 – LM	1943 – LM	1	Lanark Road	Golf halt
Haymarket	1842 – EG		5	H'ket Terr	Platforms reduced to 4
House o' Hill Halt	1937 – LM	1951 – BR	2	Corbiehill Ave	
Jock's Lodge	1846 – NB	1848 – NB	2	Restalrig Rd Sth	*See* Note 1
Joppa (1)	1847 – NB	1859 – NB	2	Milton Rd (A1)	Replaced by (2)
Joppa (2)	1859 – NB	1964 – BR	2	Brunstane Rd	
Junction Road	1869 – NB	1947 – LN	2	Gt Junction St	Previously 'Junction Bridge'
Juniper Green	1874 – CR	1943 – LM	1	Station Rd/Lanark Road	
Kingsknowe	1850s – CR		2	Kingsknowe Road	Closed 1917-9, 1964-71
Leith Central	1903 – NB	1952 – BR	4	Leith Walk/Easter Rd	
Leith Citadel					*See* North Leith
Leith North	1879 – CR	1962 – BR	2	Lindsay Road	

Name	Opened – by	Closed – by	No of p'form edges	Nearest road	Remarks
Leith South					*See* South Leith
Leith Walk	1868 – NB	1930 – LN	3	Leith Walk	Closed 1917-9
Lothian Road	1847 – CR	1870 – CR	4	Lothian Rd	Replaced by Princes St
Meadowbank	1848 – NB	c1900 – NB	1	London Rd (A1)	Also called 'Queen's' & Jock's Lodge stations
Meadowbank Stadium	1986 – BR	1988 – BR	1	Marionville Rd	Opened for XIII Commonwealth Games
Merchiston	1882 – CR	1965 – BR	2	Bonaly Place	Now Harrison Place
Morningside Rd	1884 – NB	1962 – BR	2	Morningside Rd	
Murrayfield	1879 – CR	1962 – BR	2	W Coates Terr	
Musselburgh (1)	1847 – NB	1964 – BR	1	Station Rd	
Musselburgh (2)	1988 – BR		2	Whitehill Farm Rd	
New Hailes	1847 – NB	1950 – BR	2		
Newhaven	1879 – CR	1962 – BR	2	Craighall Road	
Newington	1884 – NB	1962 – BR	2	Mayfield Gdns/Craigmillar Park	
Niddrie	1848 – NB	1869 – NB	2	Newcraighall	*See* Note 2. Closed 1860-4
North Leith	1846 – EL	1947 – LN	1	Commercial St	Closed 1917-9
Piershill	1891 – NB	1964 – BR	2	Clockmill Lane	Closed 1917-9
Pinkhill	1902 – NB	1967 – BR	2	Traquair Park E	Closed 1917-9
Portobello	1846 – NB	1964 – NB	3	Brighton Place	*See* Note 3
Powderhall	1895 – NB	1917 – NB	2	Broughton Road	
Princes St	1870 – CR	1965 – BR	7	Rutland St/Lothian Road	Temp 1870-94
Queen's					*See* Note 1
St Leonard's	1831 – ED	1860 – NB	1	St Leonard's St	Closed 1847-60
Saughton	1842 – EG	1921 – NB	2	Saughton Rd N	Closed 1917-9
Scotland St	1842 – EL	1868 – NB	3	Scotland St	
Slateford	1848 – CR	–	2	Slateford Rd	Closed 1917-9
South Gyle	1985 – BR	–	2	South Gyle Rd	
South Leith	1831 – ED	1905 – NB	1	Constitution St	
Trinity	1842 – EL	1925 – LN	2	Trinity Crescent	Closed 1917-9
Waverley	1846 – NB/E&G	–	21	Waverley Bridge	21 platforms reduced to 13
Wester Hailes	1987 – BR		2		

Edinburgh's stations: Notes

1 Four stations have existed at various times in the Meadowbank/Piershill/St Margaret's area. The first, called 'Jock's Lodge' was built east of St Margaret's Works, approximately on the site of the later Piershill Junction. It lasted only two years, until 1848, almost certainly closing when 'Queen's' station was opened (down side only) just west of the Works complex. This, possibly better known as 'Meadowbank' lasted until the turn of the century, according to George Dow. Piershill station was opened on the Abbeyhill-Piershill loop, within a stone's throw of the ECML, in 1891, and lasted until 1964. Further along what used to be the Piershill-Abbeyhill loop was Meadowbank Stadium (down side only) built for the 13th Commonwealth Games and subsequently used for a few years to transport football supporters to Easter Road Park (although not as conveniently as did the former football halt on the Leith Central branch).

2 An earlier E&D stopping place almost certainly existed at Niddrie, probably near Niddrie Mill.

3 Although Edinburgh & Dalkeith trains were picking up and setting down passengers in the Portobello (Baileyfield Road) area some 13 years before ECML trains called at the town, the North British main line station was Portobello's first, built when the line opened in 1846 and rebuilt as an island platform in June 1887. When the E&D's Niddrie-Baileyfield branch was abandoned, a sharply-graded spur was put up to the ECML from the Baileyfield (north) side, and a station opened for passenger services to and from South Leith. By the end of the century Portobello had effectively two stations totalling three platform edges. The main line station remained an island until closure in 1964, while the South Leith trains used the smaller station to the north of the main line until the end of 1904.

The author would welcome further information or corrections to the above list which is largely confined to stations within the city's boundary limits.

A key to the abbreviated company names can be found under Table 1.

2 Dalry Road Depot Allocations

1921

4-6-0
(Cl 908) 916
(918) 921

4-4-0
(66) 1124
(66) 1124
(80) 1081
(139) 932/3
(140) 140/1/3 923/4
(721) 732
(900) 889/99

0-6-0
(294) 201, 306/21, 548/54, 1548
(300) 672/3
(652) 661
(711) 330/1/2/3
(812) 278/9/90, 821/2/38/ 62/9/70/1/3

0-4-4T
(104) 106/7/8/9/67/8/9/70

0-6-0T
(272) 1509
(385) 506
(439) 384
(498) 531
(782) 254, 474/89, 516, 634, 810/1

0-4-0T
(264) 613/21/2/5

1959

4MT 2-6-4T
42270/2/3

6P5F 2-6-0
42807

5MT 4-6-0
44994 45022/3/30/36/86, 45127/55/83

2F 0-6-0T
47163

3P 4-4-0
54478

2P 0-4-4-T
55202/10/29/33

3F 0-6-0T
56312/3

3F 0-6-0
57550/9/60/5 57645/54

J35 0-6-0
64497 64500/1 64527

J37 0-6-0
64554/61/69

3 St Margaret's Depot Allocations

Class	1937	1959
B1	—	61029/99/1108/84/91 1246/60/1307/8/32/41/ 49/51/54/56/57/59/97/98
C10	9903	—
C15	9012/43	—
C16	9448/9/50/1/2 9511	67492/7
D11	6390/1/2/8/9	—
D29	9895/7	—
D30	9363/9400	62421
D31	9732	—
D32	9883/4/9/90/1/2	—
D34	9266/70/8/87 9492 9502/3/4	62471/87/88
D49	265/77/81/306/11	62711/15/18
F7	8301/8/10	—
G9	9334/52	—
J24	1897/949	—
J35	9124/9/88/9/92/9 9205/28 9347/69 9850/3/4	64462/79/82/3/9/4506/ 15/18/19/23/4/32/3/5/6
J36	9358 9648/74/80/7 9713/5/7/28/53/8/82/ 8/90	65224/58/88/327/9/34
J37	9084 9104/5/28/51/7/ 67/71 9255/72/3 9300/ 2/15 9429/37/54/63/ 70/1/2/3/8	64538/47/52/55/57/62/ 66/72/6/7/82/86/90/1/ 94/5/9/4601/3/5/6/7/8/ 12/3/24/25/37
J38	1407/14/6/7/21/2/3/ 40/2	65906/14/15/8/9/20/22/ 7/29/34
J39	2735/6/7/9	64795/4975
J69	7057 7343/56/86/92	—
J72	—	69013/4
J83	9801/3/7/10/7/23/5/7/ 30	68448/54/70/72/7
J88	9066 9114/6 9235/79/ 88 9836/41/6	68320/25/38/42
K2	4686/9/94/6 4702/3	—
K3	2471/2	61855/76/8/9/81/85/ 1900/09/11/24/28/31/33/ 55/88/90/1/2
N2	4729/39	—
N15	9020/2/47/54/65/99 9230/46/52 9387/8 9906/7/8/9/10/11/12	69133/4/5/41/4/6/9/50/ 2/4/68/73/85/6/219/22
V1/3	2897/9 2905/6/7/8/9/ 17/8/24/9/30	67610/5/7/24/49/59/66/ 68/70
V2	—	60813/18/23/25/36/40/ 73/82/83/92/94/900/31/ 33/37/53/58/65/69/71/80
Y9	9010/42 9146 9546 10083/9/90/5/7/8/100/ 1/2	68095/119
Railcars	35/6/8 31073	—
Non-LNER	—	46461/2, 47162, 78048/9

4   Haymarket Depot Allocations

Class	1937	1959
A1[1]	2564	
A1[2]	—	60152/9/60/1/2
A2	—	60507/9/10/19/29/30/34/ 35/36/37
A3	2500/2/6/8 2795/6/7	60035/7/41/3/57/87/9/90/ 94/6/7/8/9/100/1
A4	4483/4/5/6/8/91/2	60004/9/11/12/24/7/31
B1	—	61007/76/81/1178/1219/21/ 44/45
C7	714, 2193/4	
C10	9901	
D1	3051/4/7/63/4	
D11	6381/2/3/4/5/97 6400/1	62685/90/91/2/3/4
D29	9900	
D30	9411/2/4/5/6/24/8	
D34	9493	
D49	264 309	62705/9/19/43
J35	9058	
J36	9668/73 9775	65235/43
J37	9434	
J83	9813/26/8/31	68457/81
J88	9277 9844	
N15	9125 9528	69211
P2	2001/4	
V1/3	2910/5/6/20	67610/15/20
V2	—	60816/9/24/7/920/27/51/7/59
Others	—	55165

Class	1986
08	08421/515/70/1/710/8/26/30/55/61/3/4/81
20	20212/3/6/7/8/9/20/1/2/3/4/5
26	26001/2/3/4/5/6/7[3] 26008/10/11/14/15/21/23/4/5/ 6/7/8/9/31/2/4/5/6/7/8/9/40/1/2/3/6
47/7	47701-16

1   Unmodified 'A3' class. This locomotive reallocated 1/37

2   Peppercorn class   3   Class 26/0 modified for slow-speed running (for MGR operations)

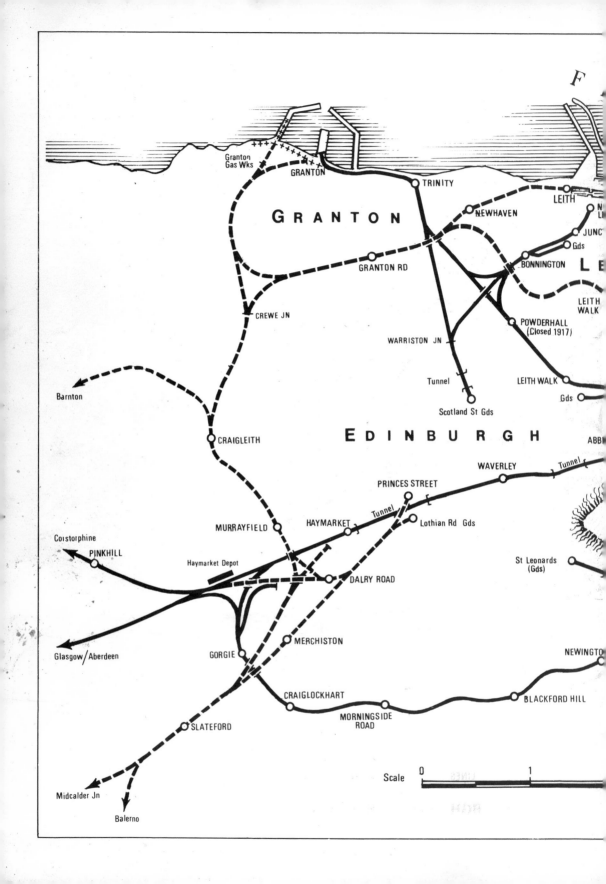